# DIVORCED FATHERS

# DIVORCED FATHERS

Children's Needs and
Parental Responsibilities

Edward Kruk

Fernwood Publishing • Halifax & Winnipeg

Editing: Brenda Conroy
Cover design: John van der Woude
Printed and bound in Canada by Hignell Book Printing

Published in Canada by Fernwood Publishing
32 Oceanvista Lane
Black Point, Nova Scotia, B0J 1B0
and 748 Broadway Avenue, Winnipeg, Manitoba, R3G 0X3
www.fernwoodpublishing.ca

Fernwood Publishing Company Limited gratefully acknowledges the financial support of the Government of Canada through the Canada Book Fund, the Canada Council for the Arts, the Nova Scotia Department of Tourism and Culture and the Province of Manitoba, through the Book Publishing Tax Credit, for our publishing program.

Library and Archives Canada Cataloguing in Publication

Kruk, Edward
Divorced fathers: children's needs and parental responsibilities / Edward Kruk.

(Basics)
Includes bibliographical references.
ISBN 978-1-55266-408-7

 1. Divorced fathers.  2. Divorced fathers--Psychology.  3. Father and child.
I. Title.  II. Series: Fernwood basics

HQ756.K783 2011      306.874'2      C2010-908061-0

# Contents

This book is dedicated to my sons, Stephan and Liam, and to all the sons and daughters who have been unjustly separated from their parents.

# Acknowledgements

First and foremost, I would like to thank the eighty-two fathers who participated in the research project upon which this book is based; the book is a testament to their strength and resiliency in their quest to be responsible fathers and responsive to their children's needs in the divorce transition, in the context of multiple barriers and impediments. These fathers rose above their trauma to contribute to a research endeavour that they hoped would have some influence on current laws, social policies and therapeutic practices that do more harm than good in regard to the integrity of the father-child relationship.

I would like to thank all the members of the research team, Natalie McCarthy, Sevitri Singh, Kathryn Sandberg, Edyta Wojcik and Bridgette Smitheram, for their exceptional work throughout the course of this project. Thanks also Nicole Conner and Adrienne Barckett of the University of British Columbia, who donated their time as valuable volunteer research assistants.

Special thanks to the steering committee for the research project, comprised of Dr. Jerry Arthur-Wong, Theo Boere, Keith Harris and Roy McIntyre. Their input was invaluable in setting the course for the project. I am grateful to the members of the Fatherhood Involvement Research Alliance, who oversaw the project, and to all my colleagues and mentors who shared their insights during the five years of this endeavour. Thanks to the Social Science and Humanities Research Council of Canada, as well as the Dean of Arts Office at the University of British Columbia, who generously provided the funding to make the project possible.

Thanks to Heather Clarry and Jill Fikowski for helping to organize the town hall meetings that were held across Canada on the results and implications of the research, and to the participants at those meetings, parents and professionals, who enthusiastically contributed their feedback on various aspects of the findings and needed directions for legal, policy and practice reform.

Finally, warm thanks to my publisher, Errol Sharpe at Fernwood Publishing, and to Candida Hadley, Brenda Conroy, Debbie Mathers, Beverley Rach and Nancy Malek, who provided outstanding advice and assistance in helping to bring the book to fruition.

# Chapter 1

# Core Issues and Theoretical Foundation

Writing, as a way of codifying human experience, sets obstacles to "reading" the inner experience of people; in the case of divorced fathers, the experience of being removed as a loving parent from the life of one's child via a sole custody order strikes at the heart of one's being. Words are inadequate tools in capturing the essence of this experience; as a divorced father, I am often rendered mute in articulating my struggles to maintain a meaningful presence in the lives of my sons and a parental identity in the face of multiple barriers and a general public indifference to my plight. This is why the stories of the eighty-two fathers who are the subject of this book are so extraordinary. Most men suffer in quiet desperation and their stories remain untold; these fathers took a major risk in coming forward and detailing their experiences of being removed as active caregivers of their children. Some of these fathers did strike out in retribution against such uprooting; most, however, sought constructive ways to stay involved in their children's lives. A few of the more activist fathers worked to bring public attention to their plight, joining in the civil disobedience efforts of groups such as Fathers for Justice.

Given the lacuna of scholarly and media reports of fathers' experiences of divorce, the story of Darrin White, which exemplifies the plight of many divorced fathers disenfranchised from their children's lives, is a notable exception to the prevalent trend. The suicide "epidemic" affecting divorced fathers is now well-documented (Kposowa, 2000), yet Darrin's is one of the few such stories that have been actually reported.

Darrin White, thirty-four, committed suicide in 2000 in Prince George, B.C., after a judge ordered him to pay his estranged wife twice his take-home pay in child and spousal support each month. Darrin wasn't a complicated man. He liked taking nature walks and enjoyed cycling, read books about the outdoors and loved animals, but mostly doted on his children. He was a certified locomotive engineer who earned his living driving trains, first for Canadian National, then the British Columbia Railway. When his marriage fell apart, he found himself in a situation shared by many men. Suddenly alone, compelled to leave his home with less than forty-eight hours' notice, denied contact with his children, expected to come up with rent money as well as lawyers' retainers, and missing shifts at work due to court dates, Darrin found himself unable to work and criticized for not paying his estranged wife child support during this chaotic period. Most importantly, it began to dawn on Darrin how vulnerable his relationships with his children, aged five, nine and ten, had now become (his oldest child, aged fourteen, from a previous relationship, lived with her mother in Saskatchewan). According to his friends, his distress revolved around an acute awareness of how much his children needed their father and his feelings of helplessness in being removed from their lives and relieved of his responsibilities as a active caregiver. No services were available to help him deal with these stresses, the court remaining indifferent to his anguish.

The media picked up Darrin's story subsequent to a multitude of testimonials attesting to his gentle and loving nature as a father and his own account of his experience prior to his death, which clearly identified legal judgments as the source of his distress. At his funeral service, his fourteen-year-old daughter spoke passionately in support of her father as "a loving and devoted father who only wanted the best for his four children," and in defiant opposition to the "barbaric" legal system which had failed him and his children. Yet when questioned about Darrin's case, former British Columbia Supreme Court Judge Lloyd McKenzie told the *Vancouver Sun*, "There is nothing unusual about this judgment" (Lee 2000), pointing out that the judge in the case applied standard guidelines for spousal and child support. The coroner's report exonerated the court as in any way responsible for Darrin's death.

The stories I have gathered for this book focus squarely on fathers' experiences of divorce, particularly in regard to their relationship with their children. The anguish they express is little different to the story of Darrin White. The fathers in my study volunteered to be interviewed about their perceptions of their children's needs in the divorce transition, their responsibilities as fathers in relation to those needs and the responsibilities of social institutions to support fathers in the fulfillment of their parental responsibilities. The fathers constituted an extremely diverse group, from a range of occupational and cultural backgrounds, some previously married and other cohabiting; thus, "divorce" is defined for our purposes as the point of physical parental separation in both marital and cohabitation arrangements.

The aims of this book are twofold. First, I seek to provide a more informed perspective on what constitutes the "best interests of the child"; to date, this elusive concept has been based almost entirely on the views of professional experts, and little is known about the viewpoint of parents themselves. Although they are the true "experts" on the matter, their voices have been excluded in current debates about the needs of children after divorce and parental responsibilities in relation to those needs. Needs are the nutriments or conditions essential to a child's growth and integrity, and for every need of children, there is a corresponding parental responsibility. In addition, the book examines the question that is overlooked in dominant discourses regarding child custody: what are the responsibilities of social institutions to support parents in the fulfillment of their parental responsibilities? "Parent blaming" rhetoric, enthusiastically applied to divorced fathers by legal and child welfare agents, is positively intended to deflect attention and accountability away from institutions such as judicial systems which routinely remove fathers as custodial parents after divorce.

The second objective of the book is to promote active and responsible fatherhood involvement after divorce and to discuss a range of socio-legal policy and practice reforms that will enable fathers to continue and enhance their parenting of their children. Fathers' own views on this question are critically examined, and I focus on what many see as the key to addressing the social problem of father absence after divorce: the shared parental responsibility framework to child custody determination. I discuss how we can make shared parenting work in the best interests of children — not just from fathers' perspective, but from the point of view of children themselves.

Fathers are no longer content to assume a peripheral role in their children's lives; a "gender convergence" with respect to child care responsibilities has emerged as a norm in two-parent families in Canada. Yet the picture changes dramatically for many fathers after divorce. Divorced fathers are faced with multiple obstacles in their quest to remain active and responsible fathers, and these barriers are not well understood. The primary barrier is the present framework of child custody determination, which needs a complete overhaul if we to effectively address the problem of father absence. In adopting a strengths-based orientation, I challenge purely psychological accounts of divorced fatherhood that are primarily concerned with enumerating men's deficits in the realm of parenting after divorce. I regard post-divorce father absence as a social problem rooted in a framework of child custody determination that removes one parent as a primary caregiver, limits parenting options within a sole custody model and discriminates against children of divorce while perpetuating an adversarial approach to dispute resolution. I challenge the dominant ideology that fathers freely choose to disengage from their children's lives and that post-divorce parenting arrangements are reflective of primary caregiver-based pre-divorce family structures. An adversarial model that conflates children's "best interests" with the competing rights of mothers and fathers, I argue, overlooks the actual needs of children in the divorce transition. A new theoretical approach, a paradigm shift, is needed beyond the dominant rights-based discourse within which child custody is presently determined; a responsibility-to-needs framework, which enumerates children's needs and parental and social institutional responsibilities vis-à-vis those needs, is required if we hope to reduce the harms attendant to divorce for children and families. Active and responsible fatherhood involvement in children's lives after divorce is a critical ingredient in such a harm reduction effort.

I have been studying fatherhood involvement and the changing role of fathers, and the problem of father absence after divorce, for almost three decades. In 2005, I embarked on the study reported in this book, in part to assess whether the situation has changed for divorced fathers and their children. To my dismay, I found that it has not substantially changed. Of the eighty-two divorced fathers interviewed for this project, thirty were struggling with a situation of parental alienation, having been completely estranged from their children's lives. It quickly became apparent to me that despite lip service about legal reforms intended to improve fathers' contact with their children after divorce, a significant number of fathers are still very negatively affected by divorce and the present system of child custody determination. In fact, the situation with regard to father absence in Canada is worse today than it was twenty years ago, when I completed my first study of divorced fathers, reported in my first book on divorced fatherhood, *Divorce and Disengagement*. In cases where parents cannot agree on parenting arrangements, the Canadian judiciary continues to award sole custody to one parent, in effect removing one parent, usually the father, as a primary caregiver from the life of a child, and this is done as a matter of routine. What has changed is the terminology, with judges referring to arrangements where children live with one parent and visit the other as "joint custody." I refer to this as "joint custody in name only" — the actual amount of time that "access parents" are able to spend with their children has in no way increased in legally contested cases of child custody.

The effects on fathers of losing their children via sole custody decrees are more pronounced today than twenty years ago — because fathers' involvement with, attachment to and influence on their children before divorce have significantly increased. This has been one of the most significant and powerful social trends of this generation. Children are now forming primary attachments to both of their parents, and the severing of these attachments have more pronounced negative effects on both fathers and children. Twenty years ago I found that fathers who lost contact with their children suffered a grief reaction containing all the elements of a bereavement. This grief, characterized by reactions of shock and denial, bargaining, anger and depression, was reported to be directly connected to fathers' experience of child absence and loss of parental identity. Today fathers are manifesting an even more pronounced reaction of post-traumatic stress, as they are acutely aware of the harms their absence is causing their children. Witnessing the suffering of their children and knowing that their children need them in their lives, and being unable to be there for their children is, according to the fathers, one of the most painful traumas a person can endure. At the same time, apart from a few self-help groups, effective support services for fathers are non-existent. And fathers mainly suffer in silence, in quiet desperation, with few people, including their own children, aware of the depths of their anguish. Those who have the courage to speak about their woundedness and their distress over the suffering of their children are subjected to a mean spirited cultural response, where all talk of woundedness is mocked.

The main difference between fathers' grief reaction of twenty years ago and the more pronounced symptoms of post-traumatic stress today, as the reader will come to see, is that the loss of one's children and the father role is a defining and organizing experience that forms the core of fathers' post-divorce identity. Arousal and avoidance symptoms are more pronounced and feelings of trauma more intrusive and persistent, and these have an impact in virtually all life domains. Thus fathers routinely report increasing isolation, loss of employment and inability to form or sustain new relationships. Twenty years ago, fathers reported a pattern of repartnering soon after their divorce and loss of their children, as new partners were often the sole source of support for these men; today, fathers are more likely to report a reluctance to become involved in new relationships. These impacts are connected to more disturbed patterns of thinking, including marked distrust of others and preoccupation with the possibility of harm ("everyone and everything is against me"), fallacies of being externally controlled and a victim of fate, shame, stigma and self-blame, and learned helplessness and hopelessness about the future. More significant impairments in fathers' psychological, social, occupational and other important areas of functioning are thus evident today than twenty years ago.

## Theoretical Orientation

As much of what we know about families, divorce and children's needs and interests has been obtained from research focused on the perspectives of professional elites working within the "divorce industry," with studies of mothers' standpoint predominating when parents' viewpoints are sought, I utilized a grounded theory approach in eliciting the missing perspective of divorced fathers on these issues. Thus, the research team designed an exploratory and descriptive qualitative study that utilized narrative inquiry as the main approach to data collection, emphasizing the importance of individual experience in knowledge construction. Our research data was approached using elements of a reflexive grounded theory approach of a constant comparative method and content analysis of fathers' perspectives. (Methodology is described in further detail in Chapter 3).

Sociological work on fathering makes it clear that fatherhood is fundamentally a social construction. The culture of fatherhood and the conduct of fathers change as social and political conditions change. In addition to a social constructivist perspective, studying fatherhood also lends itself to a systemic framework, which views fatherhood not primarily as a characteristic or behavioural set of individual men, or even as a dyadic characteristic of a father-child relationship, but as a multilateral process involving fathers, mothers, children, extended family and the broader community and its cultures and social institutions (Doherty, Kouneski and Erickson 1998). Indeed, fatherhood may be even more sensitive than mothering to contextual forces that, particularly in divorce, create more obstacles than bridges for fathers, but that potentially could be turned in a more supportive direction. With these social constructionist and systemic perspectives as a backdrop, the book examines the concept of responsible fathering and offers a conceptual framework of "responsible fatherhood" to guide social policy and socio-legal reform as well as direct practice to constructively engage fathers after divorce.

The notion of "responsible fathering" reflects a recent shift by academics and professionals away from the notion of parental rights in examining children and families of divorce (Mason 1994) toward a "responsibility to needs" conceptualization that emphasizes that for every need of children in the divorce transition, there is a corresponding parental responsibility. This viewpoint holds that parents are responsible to address their children's needs and that social institutions, as part of the larger context within which parenting is enacted, are responsible to support parents in the fulfillment of these responsibilities. Applied to divorced fatherhood, "responsible" also suggests a more explicit value advocacy approach in promoting more committed and nurturing involvement by men in their children's lives and preserving father-child attachments (Doherty, Kouneski and Erickson 1998), and ensuring social institutional support in this regard. Children need responsible and involved fathers throughout their childhood; the prime justification for promoting responsible fathering is the needs of children. At the same time, as the ethic of responsible fatherhood is essentially an ethic of care, responsibility may be seen as a need in itself. That is, fathers need the opportunity to care for others in the interests of their own well-being; the denial of responsible fatherhood is a denial of a fundamental human need. And representatives of social institutions such as the legal and child welfare systems have an ethical responsibility to foster conditions in which responsible fatherhood may occur.

How, then, is "responsible fatherhood" to be defined? Levine and Pitt (1995) have made an important start in this regard, emphasizing that a responsible father actively shares with the child's mother in the continuing emotional and physical care of their child, from pregnancy onwards. Responsible fatherhood is tied in with the notion of parent-child attachment, and thus attachment theory also informs our analysis. Levine &

Pitt also assert that commitment to the ethic of responsible fatherhood and promoting father-child attachment extends beyond the father to the mother, to professionals who work with families and, importantly, to social institutions entrusted with the support of families. Similarly, Lamb and Pleck (1985) assert that responsible fatherhood involvement is determined not only by fathers themselves but in large part by social institutional practices and supports.

Thus, our theoretical model highlights not just individual factors of paternal responsibility to children's needs but also larger contextual and structural factors of the responsibilities of social institutions to support fathers to be responsible parents. Therefore, we conceptualize divorced fatherhood as a highly contextually sensitive process, in which the undermining of paternal responsibility by representatives of social institutions induce fathers away from responsible fathering, despite their strong individual commitment. Social institutional support for fathers, on the other hand, reinforces fathers' commitment to their paternal responsibilities.

## Outline of Book

The book is comprised of six chapters. This chapter introduces the reader to the issues and provides an overview of our theoretical orientation. Chapter 2 examines what the empirical research has found in regard to the impact of divorce and child absence on fathers. It also examines the effects of father absence on children and provides a selective review of new research findings on children and families experiencing divorce, focused on research most pertinent to the father-child relationship in the context of what research suggests are the main factors associated with children's positive adjustment to the consequences of divorce. This includes studies on adult children's perspectives of their "best interests," child outcomes in shared versus sole custody homes, parent outcomes in shared versus sole custody homes and the actual involvement of parents in child care. The changing face of parenting and co-parenting in Canada is examined in both two-parent families and in the context of divorce. Chapters 3 and 4, the heart of the book, present the results of the Fatherhood Involvement Research Alliance project on separated and divorced fathers, a five-year effort funded by the Social Science and Humanities Research Council of Canada as a Community-University Research Alliance project. Chapter 3 details fathers' narrative accounts of their divorce experience, focused on their relationship with their children, and Chapter 4 examines fathers' perspectives on their children's needs and paternal and social institutional responsibilities vis-à-vis those needs. Chapter 5 discusses the social policy implications of the research, with a primary focus on the feasibility of establishing a new approach to child custody determination in Canada based on a shared parental responsibility framework. A four-pillar framework for socio-legal reform is presented.

Finally, Chapter 6 ties together the main themes of the book and includes an examination of the implications of the study for direct practice with fathers, discussing practice guidelines for service providers who wish to engage divorced fathers in a constructive therapeutic process. In addition, an overview of the equal parenting movement in Canada and in the global context is provided.

The material in this book was presented as an interactive workshop to parents and divorce professionals as part of a seven-city tour across Canada sponsored by the Fatherhood Involvement Research Alliance and the Social Science and Humanities Research Council, and the feedback from these "town hall" meetings has also been incorporated into the discussion.

# Chapter 2

# The Impact of Divorce on Fathers, Children and Families

## The Impact of Divorce on Fathers

What do we know about divorced fathers and the impact of child absence? To what degree do divorced fathers seek the opportunity to be responsible fathers to their children, and what stands in the way of responsible fatherhood after divorce?

Twenty years ago, I published the results of the first major study examining the impact of divorce on non-custodial fathers and the phenomenon of father absence, or as I referred to it then, "paternal disengagement." Various parts of the study were published in academic journals, but the whole study was reported in my book, *Divorce and Disengagement*.

The context within which that study was conducted was one in which the image of the "deadbeat dad" was how most people regarded fathers who lost contact with their children after divorce. Fathers were seen to be "footloose and fancy free" and enjoying their freedom from responsibility for child care tasks, while mothers were struggling with poverty and the psychological burdens of being solely responsible for the physical and emotional well-being of their children. A major U.S. study by Frank Furstenberg at that time (Furstenberg et al. 1983) found that 52 percent of non-custodial fathers gradually lost all contact with their children; his was a nationally representative sample and was the first to draw attention to the widespread phenomenon of father absence after divorce in North America. His assessment of absent fathers was not a positive one.

My study challenged the myth of the "deadbeat dad." I was quite surprised by some of the results of the research. The study incorporated a comparative design on two levels: a cross-national comparison of forty non-custodial fathers in Canada and forty in Britain; and a comparison of the characteristics and experiences of forty fathers remaining in contact with their children with forty who had become completely absent from their children's lives. I interviewed a wide spectrum of non-custodial fathers — occupationally, socioeconomically and ethnoculturally. For many fathers, the interview represented the first opportunity to discuss their feelings and experiences related to the divorce in a detailed and thoughtful way; in the great majority of cases, fathers were willing to share large amounts of intimate, often painfully sensitive, information.

That study, completed twenty years ago, generated a profile of non-custodial divorced fathers, particularly those who had relatively high pre-divorce involvement with and attachment to their children, as a group highly at-risk, many remaining at a high level of distress several years after divorce. The majority of these non-custodial fathers, particularly those who were involuntarily disengaged (I now prefer the term "alienated") from their children's lives, experienced a profound grieving process during and after divorce, and this grief was directly and primarily connected to the actual or threatened loss of their children. This view represented a departure from previous formulations that suggested that men's primary loss was that of their former spouse and the marital relationship; in fact, fathers were able, over time, to work through the loss of the marital relationship. Their distress was primarily linked to the loss of their children.

I found that there are three distinct aspects of fathers' grief reaction following divorce: the threatened or actual absence of their children from their lives; the loss of the parental role, which constituted the most important component of their identity (according to the research, the father role takes precedence over all other roles in the lives of men); and the constraints of the new "access" or "visiting" relationship, which in no way resembles the daily routines of parenthood — it is constricted, artificial, contained, controlled, unnatural, more like an avuncular than a parenting relationship.

The study also examined fathers' experiences with the legal system. I found a marked discrepancy between what fathers said they wanted in regard to their post-divorce relationship with their children and their actual custody and access arrangements. The legal system effectively prevented fathers from getting what they wanted, and in contrast to assertions of legal scholars that fathers who do not legally contest custody are essentially not interested in the physical custody and caregiving of their children, I concluded that the absence of a legal contest should *not* be assumed to always accurately reflect fathers' desires. Quite to the contrary of what many people assume, fathers are very interested in child custody, primarily in the form of a shared parenting arrangement, as 79 percent of the non-custodial fathers I interviewed wanted an arrangement whereby their children could live with them at least part of the time — involving some sort of daily routine where they could play a meaningful role in their children's lives and development. Fathers attributed the discouragement of legal practitioners and an unsympathetic legal system as primarily responsible for their failure to obtain the child custody arrangement they wanted. The majority of legal practitioners were described as actively discouraging alternative child custody or access options that would have facilitated an ongoing, *meaningful* father-child relationship.

The legal system is thus an important mediator between fathers' expressed desires and what they finally obtain.

Fathers also spoke of the destructive nature of adversarial legal practices vis-à-vis their subsequent relationships with their former spouses and their children. A critical factor determining the level of involvement of fathers in their children's lives after divorce is the nature of the post-divorce relationship between the former spouses; continuing conflict between the former spouses, exacerbated by legal resolution of custody and access, does not bode well for fathers' continued post-divorce contact with their children. Sixty-nine percent of fathers felt that legal practitioners and the legal system had in fact hindered the subsequent father-child relationship.

I also looked at the link between pre- and post-divorce father-child relationships. Rather than there being a positive correlation between pre- and post-divorce father-child relationship patterns, there appears to be a strong *inverse* relationship; that is, those fathers describing themselves as having been relatively highly involved with and attached to their children and sharing in child care tasks during the marriage were more likely to *lose* contact with their children after divorce (the "disengaged" fathers in my sample), whereas those previously on the periphery of their children's lives were more likely to remain in contact (the now "contact" fathers). There are thus two major subgroups of non-custodial fathers, and for each the outcome of divorce in terms of their direct involvement with their children appears to be diametrically opposed to pre-divorce patterns. While positive outcomes of divorce occur for fathers previously less involved with and attached to their children, who are subsequently able to maintain or even enhance their relationship, a large proportion of previously highly involved and attached fathers lose contact with their kids. This subgroup is the most vulnerable and at-risk population of divorced fathers. Whereas the previously less involved and attached father, faced with perhaps weekly or bi-monthly contact with his children in a "visiting" relationship, finds that with sole responsibility for his children during this time, his fatherhood role may well be enhanced; the highly attached and involved father, faced with markedly diminished contact and what he perceives to be rigid access arrangements, perhaps feeling threatened by a total loss of contact, faces a dramatic disruption from the daily routine of his former relationship with his children: an experience of child absence and role loss which, over a period of time, results in complete disengagement from the lives of his children.

The disengagement of non-custodial fathers after divorce appears to be the result of a combination of structural constraints and fathers' own psychological response to the loss of their children and the pre-divorce father-child relationship. Both structural and psychological variables are mediating factors between divorce and disengagement; combined, they are a potent force mitigating against an ongoing meaningful father-child relationship. The primary barrier to continued father involvement after divorce is the removal of fathers from children's lives via legal sole custody judgments.

Following the publication of my study of the impact of divorce and fathers and father absence after divorce, divorced fathers were suddenly "discovered" by the research community, and a plethora of studies on fathers' experiences and the etiology and trajectory of paternal disengagement subsequent to divorce appeared. For the most part, these investigations confirmed my findings and challenged the myths surrounding divorced fathers, to the point where there is now general agreement within the research community that current legal frameworks represent a significant barrier to the ongoing involvement of fathers in their children's lives, when parents themselves cannot agree on parenting arrangements after divorce and turn to the law for help (Arendell 1995; Dudley 1996; Braver 1998; Nielsen 1999; O'Neill 2002; Liete and McKenry 2002). Further, there is consensus that most fathers do not choose to absent themselves from their children's lives after divorce; their disengagement is involuntary. And the disengagement of previously highly involved and attached fathers subsequent to divorce and legal custody determinations is a pattern noted in several research studies (Fournier and Queniart 1995; Dudley 1996; Braver 1998).

More in-depth studies of the effects of child absence on fathers have appeared in recent years. These studies found that fathers are more likely than mothers to become depressed, commit suicide or develop a stress-related illness after their divorce; most divorced fathers are lonely, overwrought and disoriented, primarily because they have lost daily contact with their children (Nielsen 1999). Suicide rates are reported by epidemiologists to be of "epidemic" proportions among divorced fathers struggling to maintain a parenting relationship with their children (Kposowa 2000); and "legal abuse" has been noted as the major factor in divorced father suicide cases (Kposowa 2003). In North America, divorced fathers are nearly 2.4 times more likely to kill themselves than their married counterparts (Kposowa 2000); in the United Kingdom, divorced fathers have double the rate of death than married men (Office for National Statistics 2001). Because fathers are reluctant to let people know how unhappy and depressed they are or to ask for help, many people, including their own children, do not appreciate the extent to which they suffer the effects of child absence after a divorce (Nielsen 1999).

Researchers examining specific physical and mental health effects of child absence on fathers noted the following. Divorced fathers are twice as likely to increase their drinking compared to those who remained married; in this regard, there is virtually no selection effect, heavy drinking does not lead to divorce, divorce leads to heavy drinking (Power, Rodgers and Hope 1999). Divorced non-residential fathers are significantly more likely to smoke marijuana and to drive a car after drinking alcohol. And divorced fathers report the highest rates of unsafe sex, with 15.7 percent reporting both multiple partners and lack of condom use in the previous year, compared with 3 percent of married men and 9.6 percent of single men (Wellings, Johnson and Wadsworth 1994).

## New Research Findings on Children and Families Experiencing Divorce

Following my initial study of the impact of divorce on non-custodial fathers and child absence after divorce, a number of new research findings that pertain to children and families experiencing divorce have also appeared. These studies complement the divorced fatherhood research and challenge the practice wisdom still prevalent within the Canadian and other legal systems. This section presents a selective review of this literature, focused on studies that are most relevant to father-child relationships and of promoting responsible fatherhood involvement after divorce. These studies are a major departure from previous research still cited by government bureaucrats and policymakers and call into question present-day laws and policies pertaining to child custody and access.

Before I discuss these studies, I examine research on factors associated with children's adjustment to the consequences of divorce. Relationships with parents play a crucial role in shaping children's social, emotional, personal and cognitive development, and there is now a substantial literature documenting the adverse effects of disrupted parent-child relationships on children's development and adjustment (Kelly 2006; Lamb 2004; Lamb, Hwang and Ketterlinus 1999). This research overwhelmingly demonstrates that children who are deprived of meaningful relationships with one of their parents are at greater risk physically, psychologically and emotionally, even when they are able to maintain good relationships with the other parent. Children are more likely to attain their developmental potential when they are able to maintain meaningful relationships with both parents, whether the two parents live together or not. A large body of research documents the adverse effects of severed father-child relationships in particular, including father-infant relationships, as well as the positive contributions that fathers make to their children's development (Lamb 2004; Lamb, Hwang and Ketterlinus 1999).

Several research studies have examined what specific factors associated with divorce most trouble children. However, two groundbreaking research studies on children's needs in the divorce transition, which followed a cohort of children of divorce from childhood to adulthood, remain a key source of information about children's adjustment to the consequences of parental divorce. The main findings of Hetherington, Cox and Cox (first reported in 1978), a sophisticated study in the single-parent research tradition, and Wallerstein and Kelly (1980), which utilized the perspectives and methods of clinical research with a non-clinical sample of children and parents of divorce, overlap in several respects. Both studies found that, particularly during the first year after divorce, the parenting capacities of both mothers and fathers deteriorate significantly. During divorce and after, parents tend to ascribe their own feelings to their children and are often unaware of and relatively insensitive to their children's needs. In the midst of their own feelings of anger, rejection and bitterness, parents may not have the emotional capacity to cope with their children's feelings as well; the emotional strain engendered by the process of divorce is strongly associated with parental unresponsiveness to children's emotional needs. At the same time children often deliberately hide their distress from their parents.

Both Wallerstein and Kelly (1980) and Hetherington, Cox and Cox (1978) concluded that the absence of the non-custodial parent is a hugely significant factor in children's adjustment to the consequences of divorce. They describe the intense longing of children for their non-custodial fathers; all of the 131 children in Wallerstein and Kelly's research longed intensely for their father's return. Periodic "access" relationships between fathers and children were not sufficiently nurturing or stabilizing for either children or parents, setting the stage in the longer run for more ominous symptoms of anger, depression and a deep sense of loss among children deprived of the opportunity to maintain a full relationship with each parent. Both studies found that two factors, the degree to which children are able to maintain meaningful relationships with each parent and the amount and severity of conflict between the parents, play a major role in determining the outcome of divorce for children. Also contributing to the prolonged distress of children after divorce are children being the focus of parental conflicts, children experiencing loyalty conflicts, the poor emotional health of either parent, lack of social supports available to parents, poor quality of parenting, lack of or inappropriate communication to children about the divorce and child poverty.

Amato (2000) provided an in-depth examination of five major perspectives that have been used to account for children's adjustment to divorce. These include the absence of the non-custodial parent, the adjustment of the custodial parent, inter-parental conflict, economic hardship and stressful life changes. The most salient factor in children's adjustment, according to Amato, is the impact of inter-parental conflict. Amato proposed the development of a new "resources and stressors" model in understanding children's experience. This model suggests that children's development is facilitated by the possession of certain classes of resources (such as parental support and socio-economic resources). Also, marital dissolution can be problematic because it involves a number of stressors that challenge children's development (such as inter-parental conflict and disruptive life changes) and because it can interfere with children's ability to utilize parental resources (losing contact with one parent and access to income). According to Amato, the total configuration of resources and stressors, rather than the presence or absence of a particular factor, needs to be considered.

There has been considerable debate in the literature about the relative salience of father absence versus parental conflict in children's distress after divorce. Do children fare better in stable non-conflictual single-parent families with minimal or no contact with the non-custodial parent, or in situations where they maintain regular contact with both parents but are exposed to ongoing inter-parental conflict? In cases where conflict between parents persists after divorce, is it in children's best interests to maintain regular contact with both parents, or to limit or cease contact with one? A British study (Lund, 1987) isolated the variables of parental harmony/conflict and father involvement/absence to assess their relative impact on children's post-divorce functioning. The study utilized a large sample, a longitudinal design and multiple measures of children's adjustment. Interviewing both sets of parents (and also children's classroom teachers and others to gain an independent rating of children's post-divorce functioning), Lund divided post-divorce families into three groups: harmonious (or neutral) co-parents, conflicted co-parents and single parent (or father-absent) families. Her results indicate that children fare best in harmonious co-parental families and fare least well in single parent families. The benefits of non-custodial father involvement for children were evident in both the harmonious and conflicted co-parenting groups. Conflict between the parents was not as strong a predictor of poor outcome for children as was the absence of the father after divorce. More recently, Fabricius and Luecken (2007) have confirmed this finding.

More recent studies (Gunnoe and Braver 2002a, 2002b; Laumann-Billings and Emery 2000; Amato and Gilbreth 1999; Lamb 1999; Lamb, Sternberg and Thompson 1997; Pleck 1997; Bender 1994; Warshak 1992; Bisnaire et al. 1990) have demonstrated the salutary effects of father involvement and physical joint custody on children's divorce-specific and general adjustment. Kelly (2000), in reviewing a decade of research on child outcomes, concluded that joint custody led to better child outcomes overall and that inter-parental conflict in itself was not detrimental to children, only child-focused conflict to which children were directly exposed. Kelly and Lamb (2000) found that, almost by definition, custody and access disputes involve "high conflict" but concluded that such (non-violent) conflict in and of itself was not necessarily harmful, as conflict is inevitable in human affairs. Rosenberg and Wilcox (2006) provide an excellent overview of the importance of fathers in the healthy development of children, discussing the impact of the mother-father relationship on child outcomes, the impact of fathers on children's cognitive ability and educational achievement, and the impact of fathers on the psychological well-being and social behaviour of children. They also summarize research on the presence of fathers as a protective factor in child abuse and maltreatment of children.

When fathers are consistently involved with their children, their children enjoy better school performance, heightened self-esteem, healthier relationships with peers, healthier sex-role development, higher academic achievement and better personal success (Nord, Brimhall and West 1997; Green 2003). Such consistent involvement necessitates a daily routine where children live with, rather than "visit," each of their parents. Evening and overnight periods that children spend with each parent in co-parenting arrangements are important psychologically, according to Kelly and Lamb (2000), not only for young children and toddlers but for infants as well. Evening and overnights provide opportunities for crucial social interactions and nurturing activities that "visits" cannot provide, including bathing, soothing hurts and anxieties, bedtime rituals, comforting in the middle of the night, and the reassurance and security of snuggling in the morning after awakening. These everyday activities create and maintain trust and confidence in the parents while deepening and strengthening parent-child attachments. When mothers are breastfeeding, there is sometimes maternal resistance regarding extended overnight or full-day separations. Breastfeeding is obviously one of the important contexts in which attachments are promoted, although it is by no means an essential context, as there is no evidence that breastfed babies form closer attachments than bottle-fed babies. A father can feed an infant with the mother's expressed milk, particularly after nursing routines are well-established.

No studies have found that children in sole custody arrangements fare better overall in their psychological adjustment than children in joint custody families.

## Research on Father Absence

Just as child absence profoundly affects fathers after divorce, so father absence plays a large role in children's problematic adjustment to the consequences of divorce. It is now well-established that responsible fatherhood involvement is crucial to children's well-being, the absence of fathers in children's lives after divorce is a widespread and global social problem, and this has profoundly negative effects on children's well-being.

A major impetus for writing this book was the mounting accumulation of data on the effects of father absence on children. However, it should be noted that although it is not a subject of empirical investigation to the same degree as father absence, the absence of mothers in children's lives has similar repercussions on children's well-being. In addition, although children are negatively affected by father absence, this does not imply that the patriarchal nuclear family structure is an ideal family form; children's optimal development is evident within bi-nuclear families as well as a range of non-traditional family structures. The majority of children raised in single mother and lesbian households are well-adjusted individuals whose development is not necessarily compromised. Nor does it imply that single mothers are the cause of developmental and social problems in children. Mothers are not responsible for the effects of father absence; the devaluation of fathers is but one manifestation of the devaluation and lack of support of parents in general in contemporary culture. Rather, the data on father absence effects support a model of emergent fatherhood, in which fathers are actively and responsibly involved in child rearing, an ideal that is consonant with an egalitarian feminist agenda of a more equal division of shared parenting responsibility between women and men.

The mounting evidence on the effects of father absence, particularly in situations where fathers previously had an active role to play in their children's lives, cannot be ignored. A plethora of studies have revealed the importance of fathers in the development of children. The two major structural threats to fathers' presence in children's lives are divorce and nonmarital childbearing. Absence of fathers in children's lives, particularly after divorce, is associated with a wide range of social problems: youth crime (85 percent of youth in prison have an absent father); poor academic performance (71 percent of high school dropouts are fatherless); homelessness (90 percent of runaway children have an absent father); and fatherless children and youth exhibit higher levels of depression and suicide, delinquency, promiscuity and teen pregnancy, behavioural problems and illicit and licit substance abuse (Rosenberg and Wilcox 2006; Crowder and Teachman 2004; Ellis et al. 2003; Ringback Weitoft et al. 2003; Jeynes 2001; McCue Horwitz et al. 2003; McMunn et al. 2001; Blankenhorn 1995). Father absence through divorce is strongly associated with diminished self-concepts in children (Parish 1987), as children consistently report that they wish they had more contact with their fathers and feel abandoned when fathers are not involved in their lives after divorce (Fabricius 2003; Braver 1998; Warshak 1992). Fatherless children and youth are more likely to be victims of exploitation and abuse, and the *Journal of Ethnology and Sociobiology* recently reported that preschoolers not living with both of their biological parents (in either two-parent homes or in equal shared parenting situations after divorce) are forty times more likely to be sexually abused.

A generation of fatherhood advocates has emerged who suggest that fatherlessness is the most critical social issue of our time. In *Fatherless America*, David Blankenhorn calls the crisis of fatherless children "the most destructive trend of our generation," arguing that virtually every major social pathology has been linked to fatherless children — violent crime, drug and alcohol abuse, truancy, unwed pregnancy, suicide and mental health disorders —

all correlating more strongly with fatherlessness than with any other factor, surpassing race and poverty. Empirical studies on father absence effects confirm most of Blankenhorn's claims. After controlling for child poverty and social class, studies found that in comparison with children with ongoing relationships with both parents, father absent children:

- are more likely to suffer from short- and long-term emotional and mental health problems, including poor self-esteem, anxiety, depression, impulsivity and suicide (Meltzer at al. 2000; Hetherington 2002; Chase-Lansdale et al. 1995);
- have a higher risk of physical health problems, psychosomatic health symptoms and illness such as acute and chronic pain, asthma, headaches, stomach aches and feeling sick (O'Neill 2002; Lundbert 1993; Dawson 1991), are more likely to die as children (Lundbert 1993) and live an average of four years less over the life span (Ringback Weitoft et al. 2003; Tucker et al. 1997);
- are more likely to experience problems with sexual health, including a greater likelihood of having intercourse before the age of sixteen, foregoing contraception during first intercourse and becoming teenage parents (Ellis et al. 2003; O'Neill 2002; Wellings et al. 1994; Kiernan 1997), and to have contracted sexually transmitted infection (Wellings, Nanchanahal and MacDowall 2001);
- are at greater risk of suffering physical, emotional and sexual abuse, being five times more likely to have experienced physical abuse and emotional maltreatment (Cawson 2002), with a one hundred times higher risk of fatal abuse (Daly and Wilson 1988);
- have more difficulties with behaviour and social adjustment, more likely to report problems with friendships, experience behaviour problems and manifest antisocial and criminal behaviour (McMunn et al. 2001; Crowder and Teachman 2004; O'Neill 2002);
- have more trouble in school, scoring poorly on tests of reading, mathematics and thinking skills (Elliot and Richards 1985; Jeynes 2001; McCue Horwitz et al. 2003);
- are more likely to run away from home (Rees and Rutherford 2001);
- are more likely to offend and go to jail as adults (O'Neill 2002; Flood-Page et al. 2000);
- are more likely to smoke, drink alcohol and abuse drugs in childhood (Power, Rodgers and Hope 1999; Ely at al. 2000; Sweeting, West and Richards 1998) and adulthood (Hope, Power and Rodgers 1998);
- are more likely to play truant from school (Graham and Bowling 1995);
- are more likely to be excluded from school (Sweeting, West and Richards 1998);

- are more likely to leave school at age sixteen (Ely et al. 2000; Jeynes 2000);
- are less likely to attain academic and professional qualifications in adulthood (Sweeting, West and Richards 1998; Ely et al. 2000);
- are more likely to experience unemployment, have low incomes and remain on social assistance (O'Neill 2002; Kiernan 1997);
- are more likely to experience homelessness in adulthood (Kiernan 1997);
- tend to enter partnerships earlier, are more likely to divorce or dissolve their cohabiting unions and are more likely to have children outside marriage or outside any partnership (Kiernan 1997).

Most of these studies examined father absence in general but suggest that father absence following divorce is particularly problematic in its short- and long-term effects on children. Increasingly, however, studies have focused exclusively on father absence after divorce, isolating the effects on child well being. Parish (1987) studied the impact of father absence after divorce and concluded that father loss was associated with difficulties in children's school-based, social and personal adjustment, and diminished self-concept. Bisnaire, Firestone and Rynard (1990) found a marked decrease in the post-divorce academic performance of 30 percent of the children with absent fathers following divorce, and this was evident three years later; access to both parents after divorce seemed to be the most protective factor in academic performance, with fatherhood involvement being most influential in children's development. Drill (1986) found that when the non-custodial father is perceived as "lost" following parental divorce, children are more likely to be depressed and their perception of the non-custodial father changes in a negative direction. She also concluded that arrangements where both parents are equally involved with the child after divorce are optimal. Fabricius and Luecken (2007) examined young adults' relationships with fathers after divorce and found that poor father-child relationships and more distress associated with ongoing parental conflict predicted children's poorer health status after parental divorce and that more time with fathers was beneficial for children in both high- and low-conflict families.

Several studies have examined the impact of father absence following divorce on girls in particular. Frost and Pakiz (1990) found that girls from father absent divorced families become more involved with alcohol or drugs, reported skipping school and higher levels of depression, and described social support in more negative terms than girls from father-involved families. Lohr, Mendell and Riemer (1989) found that particular coping patterns among girls emerge in response to the absence of the father, observable during the latency years, including intensified separation anxiety, denial and avoidance of feelings associated with the loss of the father, identification with the lost object and object hunger for males. The three most commonly occurring problems were psychological distress (defined as anxiety, sadness, pronounced moodiness, phobias and depression, affecting 69 percent of the sample), academic problems and performance substantially below their ability or past performance (affecting 47 percent), and aggression toward parents (affecting 41 percent). Finally, Kalter (1987) found that among teenage and adult populations of females, father absence following parental divorce was associated with lower self-esteem, precocious sexual activity, greater delinquent-like behaviour and more difficulty establishing gratifying, lasting adult heterosexual relationships; in these cases, parental divorce typically occurred years before any difficulties were observed. Kalter noted:

> At the time of the marital separation, when (as is typical) the father leaves the family home and becomes progressively less involved with his children over the ensuing years, it appears that young girls experience the emotional loss of father egocentrically as a rejection of them. While more common among preschool and early elementary school girls, we have observed this phenomenon clinically in later elementary school and young adolescent children. Here the continued lack of involvement of the father is experienced as an ongoing rejection by him. Many girls attribute this rejection to their not being pretty enough, affectionate enough, athletic enough, or smart enough to please the father and engage him in regular, frequent contacts. Girls whose parents divorce may grow up without the day-to-day experience of interacting with a man who is attentive, caring and loving.... Without this regular source of nourishment, a girl's sense of being valued as a female does not seem to thrive.

In general, however, boys seem to pay a higher price than girls when they have little or no relationship with their fathers after divorce. Boys in father absent families are more socially immature, aggressive, delinquent, defiant and psychologically or emotionally disturbed than other boys their age, and suffer the effects of father absence in the long term (Warshak 1992; Buchanan, Maccoby and Dornbusch 1997; Biller 1993; Corneau 1991; Emery 1994; Lansdale, Cherlin and Kieran 1995). Sons are also more affected by a mother's negative opinions of her former spouse, which can do more harm to him than the lack of contact with his father (Warshak 1992). Boys are more likely than girls to become enmeshed with their mothers in ways that hurt their relationships with their fathers (Corneau 1991; Emery 1994; Wallerstein 1991). Sons also seem to be especially affected by a divorced mother's moods, depression and conflicts with fathers (Capaldi, Forgatch and Crosby 1994; Emery 1994; Wallerstein 1991).

## Children, Families and Divorce: Four Key Findings

In addition to studies on the effects of father absence on children, four key findings from three recent "benchmark" studies have appeared that further challenge present-day legal policies and practices that discourage fatherhood involvement after divorce. These studies focused on (1) children's own views about their needs and "best interests" in regard to their family relationships following divorce; (2) comparing child development outcomes and children's well being in sole custody versus shared parenting arrangements after separation; (3) comparing parental outcomes in sole custody versus shared parenting arrangements after separation; and (4) examining current patterns of child care involvement and emerging trends in allocation of child care responsibilities in families in North America.

The first study, from Arizona State University, conducted by Bill Fabricius and his colleague Sanford Braver, was a large-scale study of 830 young adult children who lived through their parents' divorces as young children. The study asked these children what they had wanted in terms of their relationships with their parents after divorce and what they considered to be in their best interests. Fabricius found that children wanted equal time with each of their parents and considered shared parenting to be in their best interests, as well as in the best interests of children generally. Seventy percent of children of divorce believe that equal amounts of time with each parent is the best living arrangement for children; and children who had equal time arrangements have the best relations with each of their parents after divorce (Fabricius 2003; Fabricius and Hall 2000). Regardless of their actual living arrangements, however — whether they lived in sole custody or joint custody homes — children said they had wanted equal time with their parents after divorce.

The researchers, in this in-depth study, compared children's actual post-divorce living arrangements with the living arrangement they wanted, the living arrangement their mothers wanted, the living arrangement their fathers wanted, the living arrangement they believed is best for children of divorce, the living arrangement they believed is best for children of divorce if both parents are good parents and live relatively close to each other, the relative number of days in a typical week with each parent they believe is best for children of divorce for children at different ages, how close they now felt toward their mothers and fathers, the degree of anger they now felt toward their mothers and fathers, the degree to which each of their parents wanted the other parent to be involved as a parent, and the degree to which each of their parents undermined the other parent as a parent. Fabricius noted the fact that although children of divorce perceive a large gender gap in their parents' generation on the issue of child custody, there was no evidence of this gap in their generation. As young adults who have lived through the divorce of their parents, it may argued that they are, in a sense, the real "experts" on the "best interests" of children of divorce. They certainly felt an injustice in not being allowed to have an equal voice in child custody proceedings. The research also found that children in sole custody homes with little or no contact with their non-custodial parent articulated feelings of insecurity in their relationship with that parent, perception of rejection by that parent and anger toward both their parents. Consistent with other research findings, children who were less close to their fathers after divorce reported worse behavioural and emotional adjustment and lower school achievement. Earlier research focused directly on children of divorce (Lund 1987; Derevensky and Deschamps 1997) had found that the absence of the non-custodial parent was the key contributing factor to children's distress after divorce.

The second key study on children and families of divorce is actually a meta-analysis of the thirty-three major North American studies over the past decade comparing child outcomes in joint versus sole custody homes. This study found that joint physical custody is associated with much better outcomes for children. Robert Bauserman (2002) compared child adjustment in joint physical custody settings with sole custody settings and also within intact family settings, and examined children's general adjustment, family relationships, self-esteem, emotional and behavioural adjustment, and divorce-specific adjustment. On every measure of adjustment, children in joint physical custody arrangements were faring significantly better than children in sole custody arrangements: "Children in joint custody arrangements had less behavior and emotional problems, had higher self-esteem, better family relations and school performance than children in sole custody arrangements" (97).

Although many of the studies reviewed by Bauserman compared "self-selected" joint custody families with sole custody families, some examined families with legally mandated joint physical custodial arrangements, where joint custody was ordered over the objections of one or both of the parents. The children in these families fared as well as those in the self-selected samples, reinforcing the findings of earlier studies that joint custody works equally well for families in which parents are in high conflict over child custody (Benjamin and Irving 1989; Brotsky, Steinman, and Zemmelman 1988). Gunnoe and Braver (2002a, 2002b), in examining child outcomes in high conflict joint custody families, found that compared with sole custody families, children in joint custody families had fewer adjustment problems, and this was not moderated by level of pre-divorce parental conflict.

Another key finding of the Bauserman meta-analysis was the unexpected pattern of decreasing parental conflict in joint custody families and increasing conflict over time in sole custody families. The less a parent feels threatened by the loss of her or his child and the parental role, the less the likelihood of subsequent conflict and violence. Alongside this finding is an earlier finding that 46 percent of first-time battering cases emerge after parental separation (Ellis and Wight-Peasley 1986; Corcoran and Melamed 1990; Hotton 2003; Johnson and Hotton 2003; Statistics Canada 2011), as these occur within the traditional adversarial forum, a "winner-loser" arena where the emotional stakes — the relationship with one's own children — could not be higher. Hawthorne and Lennings (2008) also found that limiting fathers' involvement in children's lives via sole maternal custody judgments was correlated with their reported level of subsequent hostility toward their ex-wives. Thus, the evidence is mounting that sole custody judgments increase the risk of first-time family violence; joint custody outcomes diminish it.

Finally, a Health Canada study (Higgins and Duxbury 2002) utilizing a representative sample of almost 32,000 parents found that working fathers and mothers are now almost equal partners with respect to the amount of time they devote to child care tasks, as measured by the number of hours spent in the previous week in child care-related activities, a marked departure from a decade earlier. This longitudinal study, comparing data from 1992 and 2002, found that in 2002, mothers spent an average of 11.1 hours a week and fathers 10.5 hours in child care tasks, a 51–49 percent split. Whereas father involvement had remained steady over the ten-year period, mothers' involvement had "precipitously declined," the result of longer hours spent in paid work outside the home.

Similar patterns have emerged in U.S. time budget studies (Bianchi 2000). Bianchi, Robinson and Milkie (2006) found that little disparity in the amount of time employed mothers and fathers spend with the children, and when disparities do exist, this is the result of fathers' spending more hours in paid work outside the home. Moreover, fathers are now almost as involved in routine basic care activities for their children as mothers, as opposed to strictly play activities. Bianchi, Robinson and Milkie (2006) found that U.S. fathers spend a total of 64 hours a week on all housework, child care and paid work tasks, and mothers 65; the Family and Work Institute (2007) reported that mothers spend 43 hours a week on paid work, housework and child care, while the fathers spend 51 hours; on weekdays fathers spend an average of three hours a day with their children, while mothers spend only 45 minutes more time. The more time a mother spends working outside the home, the more time the father spends with his children (Brayfield 2003; Dienhart 2002); and fathers spend more time with older children as mothers increase their paid work hours once children start school (Williams and Boushey 2010). Given their desire to spend more time with their children and their long hours at work, fathers are now reported to be as stressed as mothers in trying to balance work and family responsibilities (Milke, 2004; Winslow, 2005).

Thus, as the gender difference in time spent in child care has diminished, shared parenting is now the norm in U.S. and Canadian two-parent families, and men and women are becoming equal partners with respect to the amount of time they devote to child care (Marshall 2006). Shared child care is also emerging as the norm in the majority of divorced families where child custody has not gone to trial. Shared parenting or joint physical custody is now an option of choice for over one-third of divorced parents in Canada who are not involved in a legal contest over the custody of their children (Statistics Canada 2005), as fathers and mothers are recognizing not only the benefits of shared parental responsibility for children for each of them, but also the indispensable role that fathers play in their children's lives as active, responsible and nurturing caregivers.

Given the above findings, as divorce researcher Joan Kelly observed a number of years ago, it is ironic, and of some interest, that legal alternatives such as joint legal and physical custody have been subjected to a level and intensity of scrutiny that has not been directed toward the traditional arrangement of sole custody to the mother and two weekends each month of "visiting" to the father. The research above makes clear the potential immediate and long-range consequences for children of sole custody arrangements and "access-based" relationships. And yet, until recently, there has been no particular challenge to this traditional post-divorce parenting arrangement, nor to the power of the courts to remove parents from children's lives as routine caregivers, despite growing evidence that such post-divorce relationships are not sufficiently nurturing or stabilizing for either non-custodial fathers or their children.

# Chapter 3

# The Lived Experiences of Divorced Fathers

It is in the context of the extensive research findings pertaining to fathers, children and families affected by divorce that I undertook my second major study of divorced fathers. Unlike my earlier research on non-custodial fathers, this study was open to all divorced fathers and was based in the Lower Mainland area of British Columbia. Fathers were recruited via the Fatherhood Involvement Network of British Columbia, which is comprised of professional service providers working with fathers and representatives of fatherhood associations. This group generated the first eighteen referrals, and from there a snowball sampling method was used; a total of 150 fathers volunteered and the first eighty-two of these men were interviewed. A wide range of divorced fathers were recruited, including the "problem-oriented pole" of non-custodial fathers who were struggling to maintain their relationship with their children, sole and joint custody fathers who reported satisfying and meaningful relationships with their children, fathers who preferred and chose a traditional breadwinning role and fathers whose parental status was in a state of flux.

Both quantitative and qualitative data were gathered, using a three-part questionnaire: (1) qualitative data collection comprised of fathers' divorce stories and questions about children's needs, paternal responsibilities and the responsibilities of social institutions in regard to any perceived needed supports for fathers; (2) demographic information about the father and family, and the pre- and post-divorce father-child relationship; and (3) open-ended questions about the father and family, and the pre- and post-divorce father-child relationship. Interviews lasted between one and two hours.

To begin, fathers were asked to recount the story of their divorce in regard to their relationships and attachments with their children; they were then asked to share their perceptions of their children's needs in the divorce transition, their responsibilities to their children during that time and the responsibilities of social institutions to fathers and families undergoing divorce. In addition, they were asked what factors helped and hindered the father-child relationship during and after divorce and what were the most important issues facing them as fathers in regard to their relationship with their children after divorce.

## The Fathers and Their Stories

In regard to the demographic profile of the fathers, both previously married and unmarried as well as separated and legally divorced fathers volunteered to participate in the research. The participants were a diverse and representative group, ranging in age from twenty-five to seventy-five, with most in their forties and fifties. The mean age of the respondents was forty-seven years. Sixty of the eighty-two fathers were employed, fifty-five full-time, and employment spanned a range of occupational categories. The eighty-two fathers had a total of 182 children; they were the birth fathers of 171 (94 percent) of these children. Twenty-five of the fathers had one child and twenty-eight had two children, seventeen had three, ten had four, and two had five children; ninety-one (50 percent) of the 182 children were male and ninety-one (50 percent) were female.

Although the main focus of the research was an examination of fathers' perceptions of their children's needs and paternal and social institutional responsibilities in the divorce transition, fathers were given an opportunity to briefly recount the story of their divorce, particularly in regard to their relationship with their children. In most cases, however, fathers were keen to present a detailed account of their experience, indicating that despite extensive legal involvement in many cases, they had never been given the chance to tell their story. They wanted their full story recorded and told, to correct what they perceived to be an imbalance in existing research, to have their voice and story heard and acknowledged.

The stories of the eighty-two fathers are told below in encapsulated form in an effort to correct this imbalance. They are presented without comment, as fathers themselves requested, and provide a powerful testimony to the many structural barriers faced by fathers in their efforts to be responsible fathers and to maintain a meaningful relationship with their children. A detailed analysis of these accounts appears in the following chapters.

The synopses below are summarized accounts of fathers' stories of their divorce experiences, particularly in regard to their relationship with their children, compiled by three members of the research team.

### 1. Joe

Joe and his wife separated ten years ago. They had three children, twin boys age seven, and a daughter, age eight at separation. His wife did not let him see the children, and they were told he threatened to kidnap them. It took two years to go to trial and by then, his children did not want to see him. He was awarded access to his children, but his wife did not abide by the order. Supervised access was then ordered. Joe missed many life events with his children. His wife changed their son's surname.

Joe contacted a number of mutual aid men's groups but did not find them very helpful. He did some reading about parental alienation and reconnecting with children on his own. He is trying to slowly rebuild his relationship with his children. He feels he has been financially ruined during the course of the legal process.

### 2. David

David and his wife separated over ten years ago after a two-year marriage, when the children were six and two. They divorced because of conflict over money. He lost contact with both children and did not see them for almost ten years. His wife moved away taking all the family finances and possessions. David went through many court appearances, with about twenty judges; police were also involved in his case. His ex-wife falsely accused him of abuse. During the past ten years, David has been unable to obtain any information about his children, including their educational progress or medical condition.

David has a very negative image of the legal system, especially in regard to gender-based inequality and the differential treatment of mothers and fathers. His ex-partner has not adhered to any of the court orders to date, and the court has been unable to address the issues of access denial and parental alienation.

After ten years, David was able to re-establish contact with his children on his own, and with the help of a psychologist. Currently he sees his kids two out of three weekends, and 50 percent of all holidays, although he would like much more, and a recommendation of a psychologist was for more than that (every weekend, every Wednesday, and 50 percent of all holidays).

### 3. Bruce

Bruce and his wife separated twelve years ago after a seven-year marriage. Their daughter was two and a half and son one year old at the time. Bruce initially saw his children every weekend and on Wednesdays. The mother developed a severe alcohol problem and Bruce decided to pursue sole custody. The court process was lengthy; Bruce ran out of money for lawyers and represented himself in Supreme Court. He was awarded fifty-fifty custody initially but gradually the children began to live with him full-time. Eventually, Bruce was awarded legal sole custody. Currently, the children's mother lives nearby but has little contact.

Bruce is happy with his current situation but remembers the divorce process as the darkest time of his life. He was off work for fourteen months during the lengthy court proceedings.

### 4. John

John and his wife attended counselling and saw a psychiatrist in order to plan their separation, following a nineteen-year marriage. However, he came home one day to find that his wife had emptied the house of its contents and had left with the children. Their two daughters were fourteen and twelve at the time, and their son was nine.

It took months to get to court. John spent $55,000 in the process. He was awarded joint custody but his wife would not comply with the court order. John called the police to enforce the court order, but they would not intervene. John feels that his wife has turned the children against him by repeatedly saying negative things about him. His daughters refused to speak with him for many years; he retained a relationship with his son by phone and infrequent visits. He feels his son has been emotionally hurt because of criticism by his mother and sisters for keeping in contact with his father.

John did not have the emotional or financial resources to return to court to have the custody order enforced. He has undergone treatment for severe depression and has at times been unable to work. He has been gradually increasing his contact with his son.

## 5. Brad

Brad and his wife separated two years prior after a nine-year relationship (including a five-year marriage). They had marital counselling for six months and then a trial separation. Their daughter was two years old at the time of the separation, and Brad's wife was pregnant with their second child. Brad describes verbal, psychological and physical aggression toward him at the end of the relationship, and he decided to leave the family home to shield his children from the marital conflict and their exposure to his wife's abuse toward him.

The couple attended mediation in an attempt to reach an agreement out of court. Brad feels that the concessions he made in mediation set the stage for future demands by his wife. He felt that the mediators (a married couple) were biased and pressured him to make concessions, which gave the mother the upper hand. An initial court order permitted Brad's wife to relocate to another province and stay with her family for the birth of their second child (a son). Brad was not permitted to attend the birth. His wife was away for four months, during which he was allowed one week per month with his children.

After Brad's wife returned home, a ten-day custody trial took place. His goal was equal parenting time, but the court awarded joint guardianship with primary maternal residence. For Brad this was essentially the equivalent of sole maternal custody. Brad's wife now wants to relocate out of province permanently, and they will have to return to court on this matter. Brad sees his daughter every other weekend and one day per week. His access to his son has been limited to one or two hours each week but is slowly increasing. Brad expresses a strong desire to be much more involved in his children's lives.

## 6. Tom

Tom and his wife separated almost two years ago, when his wife told him she wanted to end the relationship. Tom moved out of the family home. The separation came as a surprise to Tom, who did not think that there were problems in the marriage. The couple have one son who was two years old at the time of the separation. For six months after the separation, the couple and son continued to do activities together.

Tom's wife works full-time shift work. He has been on medical leave from work since two months after the separation and has not returned to work. Tom and his wife live within five minutes of each another. He takes care of his son, mainly during the day, for about half the time. He feels that he has a close bond with his son.

The couple is not legally divorced. They have met with a mediator but court proceedings have not been initiated. Tom would like to keep it out of court. He currently pays child support voluntarily; he believes that this helps to ensure his access to his son. Tom feels his wife underestimates and undervalues him as a parent, but overall he is happy with his current level of access.

## 7. Preston

Preston and his common-law partner were together for ten years. They had difficulties in the relationship and stopped living together in 1994, the same year their first son was born. Preston felt that his partner was manipulative and controlling. The relationship ended in 1997, while she was pregnant with their second son.

Preston started a new relationship in 1997 with a woman to whom he is now married. He fought for access to his sons for seven years. He says that his children's mother made false allegations of physical abuse, accusing him of abusing his sons. Because of this, he took a polygraph test and endured a two-month police investigation. He is angry that his ex-partner was not held to account for lying. He, on the other hand, had to live with supervised access arrangements.

For two years he saw his second son only once. He went without seeing his first son for over a year at one point. His ex-partner has sole custody and there is joint guardianship. Currently he sees his sons twice a month for two days each time. Ideally, he would like to have the kids 40 percent of the time. He works a flexible schedule (being self-employed), and does not understand why his ex-partner uses babysitters when the children could be with him.

His career was impacted, and he had significant legal expenses. His former partner, a trained nurse, went on social assistance and used legal aid.

## 8. Lloyd

About four years ago, Lloyd and his wife went through an emotional crisis when his wife was diagnosed with cancer. After an eighteen-year relationship, she asked him to leave the family home. He had been the stay-at-home parent with his two sons for thirteen years. He decided that it was not going to be good for the children to pursue a lengthy, bitter court battle so he gave up all rights to child custody and child and spousal support, and now only sees his children periodically. They are now teenagers. Lloyd tries to give them a choice rather than forcing them to see him every second weekend, which is what the separation agreement, negotiated via mediation, stipulates. He tries to be available to them by cell phone whenever they should need him. He lives within walking distance of his sons' home.

## 9. Brian

Brian and his ex-wife have four daughters, seven to sixteen years of age. His ex-wife had an affair with her future boyfriend, with whom she moved in, and took the children. Since then Brian's access to the children has been strictly limited. He indicated that the courts had the power to place the children with both parents, yet gave all rights and decision-making power to the mother. One daughter, who is autistic, has been living in a special needs placement away from home. He has difficulty getting to see the children because of court decisions which gave the mother full discretion as to whether and when the father could see them. Brian lost his job, has not had a relationship with another woman for a while and feels he should be able to see the children whenever he can. He believes that the children have been alienated from him by the mother and feels powerless do anything about this. He is estranged from his children at this time. Brian left the interview crying.

## 10. Craig

Craig, a young man who has one son, now fourteen, decided to move out of the family home and rent a suite, while he and his wife attempted to solve their problems. After he left, the locks were changed, and he lost access to both his child and his home. Numerous court appearances have failed to correct the problem of access denial. He feels that his wife, who refused to obey the court order and allow him access to the child, should be legally held to account. He lives with his father, who supports him financially, as he is not able to pay his bills. He has done only odd jobs since his divorce, whereas before he had a steady income. His health has suffered due to the distress in his life. His wife is in a new relationship, and this makes access even more difficult for him. He has been able to bring his son to his father's residence for short periods of time. His emotional state has improved because of the support he gets from the local men's resource centre.

## 11. John

John has two children, a daughter thirteen years old and a son nine years old. After he separated from his former partner, he moved from Vancouver to Vancouver Island. In the beginning, he had the children 40 percent of the time. Currently, the children are able to visit his home but not on a regular basis. His wife decides when he can see the children and has over time alienated them from their father.

John said he wanted to make a contribution to the research project in order to further changes to the way the family divorce cases are handled in court. He felt that he could not make adjustments to his work situation that would allow him more time to be with his children because he would be penalized for this by the court; the court would look at any decrease of income as a tactic to pay less child support. He sees divorce as an industry that is primarily profit-oriented and little concerned with the needs and welfare of children. He is hopeful that the court will make better decisions when he attends his upcoming hearing for increased access.

## 12. Paul

Paul has been embroiled in the court system for over three years. He has lost his career and his home and has not seen his three girls for over two years. He was charged with spousal abuse after he pushed his wife away when she kept pulling him back when he tried to leave the family home. He was removed from his home and charged with assault, resulting in a no-contact order. His children are young, and he has not seen them since this incident. He is emotionally upset and has suffered ill health since the separation three years ago. He cannot go to his children's school or attend any school functions in which his children are involved. He is living in a friend's mobile trailer since he was removed from his home. His daughters are alienated from and hostile toward him. He feels helpless in his situation, saying that his life been taken away from him and he does not know what to do.

## 13. Bill

Bill has three boys, age twenty-five, fifteen, and twelve, and one daughter, age seventeen. He does not get to see them very much as he lives out in the country, whereas the mother and children moved to the city after the separation. They had a separation agreement which was later ratified by the court. She told him that he could see the kids regularly, but she has not kept her word. Bill feels that his ex-wife has alienated the children to the point that they think that he is not good enough for them. Although he has legal joint custody, he is not able to see the kids very often.

Bill would like to have more access to the children but feels alienated by his ex-wife and the courts and states that there is insufficient legal or social support for fathers like him, who want to be involved in their children's lives.

All he wants is the freedom to be with his children. He would like to see more equitable sharing in the custody of children, especially as this is a family and not a criminal matter.

Bill is also estranged from his son from his first marriage, whom he has not seen in many years. He describes his situation as one of learned helplessness in regard to his relationship with his children; he feels powerless in the face of access denial and the lack of support from the legal system.

## 14. David

David has four children, one daughter age twelve and twin sons age eight, and a five-year-old son. He was married for almost twenty years. His ex-wife was a nurse in a correctional facility, where she became romantically involved with one of the inmates. David ended the relationship at that point, sought full custody of the children, in the end compromising at equal shared parenting, provided that the court order prevented the inmate from having any contact with his children, and that she would not have any contact with the inmate. He utilized the services of a mediator and had good results, as both parties were cooperative in the negotiation process. He now has equal physical custody, with no child support being paid as both parents earn about the same amount. He has a good relationship with his children, and remains friendly with his ex-wife, because he was able to negotiate a structured shared parenting arrangement with both parents having routine contact with the children. He thus feels that his experience is quite different from other fathers.

David was very interested in telling his story so that people could hear that not all divorce cases involve a hostile battle and that positive outcomes are possible.

## 15. David

David has one son and divorced when his child was six. He felt that he could not get as much access to his child as he wanted because of the court ruling in his case. His former wife did not allow free access, and he was prevented from taking his son out of the country to visit with his relatives in England. He lost his assets in the legal process and had to pay unreasonably large child support payments, which left him with little money to buy furnishings for his home or for necessities for his child; he feels he was prevented from making a home for his child because of high child support payments. According to David, the courts should have less authority in family matters, and both parties' parental rights should be equally respected. His son, now twenty-four, decided to live full-time with his father at age sixteen. David has not gotten into another relationship because he is afraid that this will come between his child and himself.

### 16. Keith

Keith has two children, both girls, now fourteen and seventeen. The parents separated when the girls were young, sharing custody equally and living in close proximity. Keith's wife, unhappy with the joint custody arrangement, took the children out of the country for an extended period of time, broke contact, and he could not find them. He did get the Canadian Missing Children's Bureau involved and they were a good support to him. They helped him to eventually locate the children and were able to re-unite him with them. At that time he went back to court and received sole custody; however, his wife was able to get the decision changed to joint legal custody with primary residence with mother. The children have been with their mother since then, with Keith getting access, as determined by the court; however, his wife still makes the decisions as to whether or not the children can see their dad. At the present time, his wife is more financially secure than he is, but he is still making child support payments in the same amount as set before. His children now live in two locations (Canada and the U.S.) and are able to travel freely with their mother; however, he has to get permission in order to take them out of the country to visit with his family in England.

### 17. Paul

Paul has a unique situation in which both parents were able to work out their post-separation parenting arrangements and viewed the welfare of the child as the main priority, rather than their own differences. They have one son, age four at the time of separation and now a teen, who is able to spend as much time as he likes between the parents and can request where he wants to be at any given time. It is an exceptional case in which court hearings were avoided. The parents settled everything with the help of a mediator and abide by respectful rules. Paul's wife is in a new relationship, and her partner is actively involved in parenting Paul's son as well, which does not bother Paul in any way. Paul is not in a relationship at present because he feels that this may jeopardize his relationship with his son.

### 18. Theo

Theo separated from his former partner twelve years ago when his son was five and his daughter two. His ex-wife moved from Surrey with their kids to Vancouver Island. At that time she did not allow him any access. Theo believes that her lawyer precipitated a number of destructive actions, such as advising her not to allow him to see the kids. That was only the beginning of the "war" between him and his ex-wife. His ex-wife has completely controlled his access to the kids. After a period of access denial by mother, he managed to negotiate supervised visits, which he did not like but agreed to under duress (he could either agree or not see the kids). Theo states that his relationship with his children has always been of primary importance to him. He eventually went to court to fight for access.

The parents eventually found a mediator who was very unhelpful. The mediator did not write down their agreements and did not get them to "sign off." After the mediation, Theo's ex-wife started to disparage him to the children (she was sharing all the aspects of their disagreement with the kids from her point of view). In consequence, his children, especially the son, became angry with him. Currently, Theo is having better contact with his children. He has also volunteered for the school's parent advisory council, became the treasurer and volunteered to sit in on the children's classes once a week to help other students.

## 19. John

John and his partner separated during the first year of their son's life. Although he wanted to establish a stable parenting schedule for his son (he initially looked after his son for two and a half days per week), he conceded to the mother's fluctuating schedule for fear of losing his son altogether. Also, as a recent immigrant from the U.S., he was not employed and struggling financially on income assistance.

After two years, he found employment and gradually increased the time he had with his son. The court did not become involved until seven years later. However, when the situation was brought before the court, he tried to keep things amicable and not try to gain custody for fear of losing what he had. For the last five to six years, the parents have been sharing time with their son almost equally. Things have become more difficult since the mother remarried and moved away. The father's involvement in his son's school, sports and other activities has declined. The new school is not sharing any information about his son with him.

## 20. Brian

Brian had two children with different partners. The first marriage ended amicably and resulted in equal shared parenting of his daughter from the time of separation, when his daughter was age five until age sixteen. The relationship is still amicable despite the fact that his daughter now lives full-time with her mother. The mother of his second child, however, was physically abusive toward him, yet she charged him with assault. He was conditionally discharged, and after separation had less than 40 percent care of his son. She remarried and moved an hour away, reducing his parenting to less than 20 percent time.

His son (now ten years old) wants to live with his father; he believes that the mother is abusive to their son, both physically and emotionally. Brian is very angry toward the court system, with a critical political and social analysis of the "divorce industry."

## 21. John

John divorced four years ago when his children were eight and four. John moved out of the family home and set up a parallel living space nearby. The parents shared parenting, four days on and four days off. This situation deteriorated when both parents remarried and relocated. Their daughter started having anxiety attacks, and their son started to become alienated from the father. Increasing acrimony between the parents and distance resulted in a communication breakdown that compromised the shared parenting arrangement. Despite John's attempts at negotiation, the mother did not take steps to ease the situation, despite the recommendation of the daughter's psychiatrist. The son developed behavioural problems. Currently, there is a marked lack of communication between the parents, lack of facilitation of John's access and lack of parental expectation around rules, structure and parenting practices. The children essentially live in two cultures, enjoying a much higher standard of living in their mother's household. Things improved somewhat after John and his new partner had a child, with whom the children are closely attached. However, after another brief period of shared parenting, the children now reside full-time with their mother.

## 22. Jim

Jim has three children age fifteen, thirteen and twelve. He has not seen his eldest child in three years, the others in two years. He reluctantly agreed, under pressure by his lawyer, that mother could have sole custody, but only later realized the full legal consequences and ramifications of relinquishing custody. At first he had the children every second weekend, with a court order for twice-a-week phone calls. The mother subsequently promoted and instilled parental alienation. She made false allegations that he was stalking the family. He arranged a third-party neutral site for visitation but the children did not show up.

Jim has spent $43,000 on legal fees and been to court seven times, resulting in seven court orders in his favour, but mother has not complied with these orders. Currently, he is completely excluded from his children's lives.

## 23. Robert

Robert and his wife decided to separate and attended separation counselling. He was falsely accused of physically harming the children (a minor injury of his child resulted in temporary child welfare involvement). His lawyer assumed an adversarial stance toward child protective services, which escalated and became a big problem for Robert. The whole process became very stressful for all family members, especially the children. Robert is concerned that his ex-wife routinely takes the kids out of the country without his knowledge. The police do not get involved because this is a civil matter.

He is very emotionally upset about the whole process. He does not receive report cards or information from the school because he is not a primary caregiver. Everyone in the family is suffering. He has been hit hard financially by the separation.

At the conclusion of the child welfare investigation, Robert obtained shared custody, but because of various obstacles, this has deteriorated to about four access days a month.

### 24. Stephen

Stephen's wife had an affair. She packed and left the family house, her husband and three kids for four days. After that, she made a list of her demands but changed this three times in one week. In court, Stephen obtained a "joint custody" order, in the form of joint guardianship; however, "primary residence" with the mother has kept the conflict going. Legal fees have exhausted his life savings.

Stephen feels that his wife wanted primary residence only because of the monetary advantage this gave her. Current parenting arrangements are in flux, and the uncertainty about their living arrangements has created stress for the children, resulting in the emergence of health problems.

### 25. Hal

Hal's divorce proceedings started after his son indicated to a counsellor at school that dad "frightened him," and child protection services became involved, leading to the separation and a court battle over access to his two adopted children. Following his admission to a psychiatric unit for depression, his access was denied for a period of time, and then supervised access was ordered.

Hal indicates that he spent lots of money on lawyers and court hearings; he lost his job. Despite a psychological assessment recommending sole maternal custody, through extensive applications to the court and his children's stated wishes to be with their father, he now has equally shared custody of his kids.

### 26. Jim

Jim indicates that during the marriage his wife was an abusive, violent offender. Despite her unreciprocated assaults on him, she enlisted the help of a battered women's shelter and left with their infant son, and he lost contact. Eventually he obtained court-ordered access, with access supervision by his parents. He has been to court sixty-two times, has been through twelve legal aid lawyers and ended up learning about child custody law and representing himself. His wife lied to the court without any consequences. She did not adhere to court orders, again with no consequences.

After long battles in courts, spending many thousands of dollars proving his wife's drug abuse and attendant neglect of their son, Jim obtained sole custody of his son. In addition, the court ordered baptism in the Catholic faith and preschool attendance (his son is the only child in Canada who has ever been court-ordered to be baptized). His son's mother has completely disengaged from her son's life, and Jim has been unable to find out her whereabouts.

### 27. Wren

About three years ago, Wren's wife decided that she was no longer heterosexual and was destined to live as a lesbian. On the condition that he move out of the house, Wren was able to see the kids, a girl and a boy, whenever mother was working. However, over the last four years his former partner has tried to eliminate all significant contact between him and the children. Even though their separation and custody agreement specifies that they have joint guardianship, his ex-wife does not consult him on any of the decisions made about the children (their education and medical care).

Wren feels that his custodial rights are not being respected. His former partner does not honour any of the court-ordered access time or other stipulations. He has been back to court repeatedly regarding the issue of access denial, with no successful resolution. Even his limited access time has been reduced by the court. According to Wren, even if you are a saint, lawyers will always find something to use against you in court.

### 28. Yimin

Yimin has one child, a boy age nine. He states that his ex-wife used to physically abuse their son very often. He tried to talk to the school counsellor about the situation but he did not help, and no one wanted to inform the school and the police. According to Yimin, there was no help available from the community, no one wanted to listen. Finally, child protection services were called, and Yimin told the child protection worker that his wife was physically abusing their child. They asked the mother to leave the home, but she refused to do so. As a result, their son was taken to a foster home. The child protection worker told Yimin that his son would be returned if Yimin could demonstrate that he could provide a safe home for him. When he went to court on the matter, the social worker did not appear; he went to court three times and each time social worker did not show up. As a result, the court said there was no evidence of maternal unfitness and only the abusive mother was given access to the son.

During this lengthy process Yimin lost his job, his business claimed bankruptcy, and his lawyer quit his case. Eventually the mother disengaged from her son's life, and Yimin was able to restore contact. Currently Yimin lives with his son; the mother has not seen her child in three years.

## 29. Darrell

Darrell was dating a young woman who became pregnant, although her doctor had said she was unable to conceive. She gave birth to triplets, and the period immediately following the birth was an extremely stressful and challenging time for the couple. Darrell was very supportive of both mother and the children, who had to remain in hospital for an extended period. After three months, the babies were ready to leave the hospital. Darrell came to the hospital to learn that the babies and his girlfriend were gone. It took six months to locate them. The mother of the boys put "unacknowledged" for "father" on their birth certificates, and this subsequently created much trouble for Darrell. He states that he literally has had no rights as a father.

Darrell fought hard to change this situation. The BC Supreme Court started investigating the case. In the end, he was ordered to pay support payments totalling more than his actual salary. His former girlfriend brought forward a number of unfounded allegations; she lied to court about him.

After consulting with over forty lawyers over four years, who all refused to help him, Darrell found a freshly minted junior lawyer who was willing to help. He applied to the BC Supreme Court, failed, then went to the BC Court of Appeal, again without success. Darrell then appealed to the Supreme Court of Canada to fight for his rights as a father. Finally, after six years of litigation over the matter of paternity, the Supreme Court of Canada unanimously agreed that he was discriminated against based on gender, under section 15 of the Charter of Rights and Freedoms. The court ruled that the B.C. government had one year to change the paternity law so he would be acknowledged on his children's birth certificate (a clause that says that with children under seven, the dad automatically has his name added on the birth certificate and the children would carry a joint surname). To date the B.C. government has not complied. He is allowed access about four times a year, four to five hours at a time, at this point.

## 30. Brent

Brent knew the mother of his child for one month before she got pregnant. About six months into her pregnancy, she became violent and continued this behaviour after the birth of the child. Fearing the effects of his daughter's exposure to her mother's physical and verbal abuse of him, Brent left the relationship when his daughter was one year old. This was followed with Brent being falsely accused and a charge of assault being laid against him, which resulted in a restraining order against him. After that, access to his child was repeatedly denied, and court orders for access not adhered to. After seven court appearances on the issue of access denial, the mother agreed to comply with the access order. The judge was satisfied; however, she again did not follow through. The judge subsequently simply told the father that she has a court order for sole custody and is expected to comply with access. However, she has not complied with access provisions, with no legal consequences.

Currently, the mother and daughter live on Salt Spring Island; his access is mostly denied or limited and constrained by the mother. Brent has not given up in his quest for a meaningful relationship with his daughter.

### 31. Michael

Michael's former partner left him eight months ago with his children. Before the separation, they went through marriage counselling. There had been disagreements about safety issues of the baby sleeping between two of them, which she wanted but he opposed. Also, Michael used to travel a lot for work-related matters, and he was absent from home for days at a time. Finally, the issues of child safety and his wife's physical abuse escalated, to the point of his wife leaving. The precipitating event took place when he threw a book against a wall and the police were called, although no charges were laid against him. One month after that incident, he came home to discover that his wife and children were gone, with family possessions removed, and money taken from the bank account. Access to his children was denied for three days.

Currently, he sees his children four days a month. The mother constantly criticizes the father in front of the children, and he remains concerned about their safety and wellbeing.

### 32. Robert

Robert has two daughters with different mothers. In the case of his first child, separation occurred after the mother moved to Calgary with their daughter. When she came back, Robert was given weekly access from Friday to Sunday. A subsequent court decision changed the access from Saturday to Sunday only. The court also ordered joint guardianship, allowing Robert access to medical and school information and telephone access every day. However, the child's mother repeatedly broke court orders. He had to fight to receive any information about his daughter.

In the case of his second child, Robert's wife left with their child after accusing him of sexual assaulting their daughter. Robert lost all access to his child as a result. Police investigation proved the father innocent, and no charges were laid. The mother then moved to Vancouver Island. Robert now sees his daughter every second weekend for three half days. He has been fighting for sole custody of younger daughter for three years.

### 33. Alan

Alan has two daughters, age twenty-four and nine, with two different women. In the first case, he was a very young father; there were many disagreements with his wife about parenting matters. His daughter was five when her parents separated. In the beginning, the paternal grandparents helped the couple with the daughter; after the separation they took the child to live with them. They tried to keep the child away from the parents' conflict; however in the process they actually exacerbated the conflict and alienated their daughter-in-law. With the help of the RCMP, the mother, who had obtained an ex parte court order, removed the child from the grandparents' care, and the girl went to live with her mother.

A court order for paternal access was routinely ignored by the mother, and eventually, Alan's access to his child was denied altogether. His daughter now is twenty-four; he has little or no contact with her. His daughter is firmly allied with her mother and a staunch advocate of sole custody.

In the second case, he was the full-time caregiver of his daughter before the divorce. When the daughter was four, his wife decided to leave, and she took the child away with her. In the beginning months of the separation, there was a joint custody agreement, which worked well for Alan but not for his ex-wife. Following a disagreement regarding division of assets, she applied for sole custody, which she received, and from that point did not want to cooperate with him. He decided to apply to the BC Supreme Court for a variance to the sole custody order, asking for joint custody and equal co-parenting, but got an enforcement order for specified access instead. His ex-wife denied all access after that time, and from that point the circumstances of his second separation paralleled those of his first. In fact, the two ex-wives met and colluded in excluding him from his daughters' lives.

He has been fighting for equal parenting and joint physical custody for three years and ten months, during which time he has not seen his daughter. He has numerous personal and professional testimonials attesting to his capacity as a father and primary caregiver.

### 34. Jamie

Jamie's marital relationship deteriorated over his frequent absences from home for his job. He has three kids, a son five years old and two daughters, four and two years old, with whom he now has a good relationship. He separated from his wife not knowing that she was pregnant with their third child. When he found out, he decided that he did not want to get back together just for the sake of the child. His ex refused him visitation; therefore, he had to go to court for access. Even after access was granted by the court, she would not answer the phone on his weekends to go visit the kids. They decided to get a divorce, but she remained adamant that he was not going to see the children. They went to court over the issue of access denial; she did not have legal representation and was informed that she could not deny access. She has since respected the access order.

Jamie now has joint custody of his children. He also has had another child with a new partner (since separated), with whom he has good contact. His second ex-wife did not create any problems regarding contact.

### 35. Robert

Robert's ex-wife slept with her future boyfriend, for whom she left the marriage. She and Robert had two children together, a boy age ten and girl seven years old at separation. Child custody was equally shared; in fact, Robert had the kids six out of every eight days for six months before he had to move from Prince Rupert to Vancouver because of a job transfer. His ex-wife then moved to Vernon, where he was able to see the kids for two days per week. In the meantime, he met another woman, whom he married. After he remarried, he was transferred to Kamloops, closer to the kids. There were a few "head games" around child care and access. His ex-wife wanted to control his access to the kids; she still phones their daughter every day when she is with him and tries to control his activities with the daughter.

In the end, things worked out well for Robert. He now has joint custody of his children. He also has had two more children with his second wife. However, animosity between the parents and the rigidity of the legal system has left him angry and frustrated. Before the joint custody order, his relationship with his children was extremely strained, due to the stresses attendant to the legal process.

### 36. Brian

Brian and his ex-partner were together for a very brief period, during which she became pregnant with his child. She was not interested in father involvement in her child's life because he was not living with her. She denied him all access to his child, and he eventually married another woman. His son contacted him at age nine. By then his son was in the care of child protective services, which had sent a letter to Brian indicating that he had three days to "claim" that he was the father. Currently, the mother of his child is in Indonesia; she had been in and out of the boy's life. His son has not seen mother in three years. Brian is overwhelmed by the process of legally adopting his child. He must find a lawyer, fill out the paperwork properly. On top of that, his legal fees are very expensive; government agencies are not very helpful.

His son is now living with him while the mother remains out of the country. He has had two children with his new wife, and his son has integrated well into the new family.

### 37. Keith

For seventeen years, Keith was happily married, with three children, fourteen, twelve, and ten years of age at separation. However, when he went away to start work for the season, he received a divorce application. During the initial separation, he had very limited access to his kids. There were accusations by the mother against Keith regarding child and spousal abuse. The court ordered a psychological assessment of the whole family. The custody and access assessment recommended reasonable paternal access to his boys, but none with his daughter. At that time Keith made a formal complaint to the College of Psychologists regarding the assessment. Throughout the process of establishing access, Keith's relationship with all of his kids severely deteriorated. The mother retained the matrimonial home as this was argued by her lawyers to be in the best interests of the children. Four years later, however, the mother's law firm foreclosed on the house in order to recover their legal fees, and the mother and the children lost their home.

### 38. Dave

Dave's ex-partner decided to break up their relationship. Two weeks after the break-up, she phoned to inform Dave that she was pregnant (her fourth child and his first). She also told him not to come around to see the child or she would get the police involved, saying that he had harassed and abused her. Dave was allowed very limited contact with his son; he got only forty hours in his son's first year. His son is now three years old; during the last two years, Dave has had no contact. As there has been no court involvement, all access is determined solely by the mother of the child. Dave feels powerless to correct the situation, as he believes he has little chance of success within the legal system.

### 39. Wayne

Wayne and his ex-partner separated before the birth of their child. The mother repeatedly denied access to their daughter, including court-ordered supervised access at an access centre. Finally, after 180 denials, Wayne obtained an enforcement order. This was huge news in Hamilton where the trial took place. The mother went to jail for denying access and not complying with court orders.

This case has been fraught with high conflict from the beginning, including physical violence toward the father, unsubstantiated allegations of child sexual abuse and the involvement of child protection services. The problem of access denial did not abate, despite the mother's incarceration. Emotionally devastated, Wayne has not seen his daughter since 1998. The mother continued to deny access regardless of the previous consequences.

### 40. Jeff

Jeff lived in a common-law relationship for nine years. The couple has two children: a three-year-old boy and a six-year-old girl (one and four at separation). After they separated, she became the custodial parent, and he experienced challenges in his attempts to visit his kids. Jeff routinely had to remove himself during access visits rather than expose his kids to scenes of parental conflict. There were also times when he was prevented from seeing his children, for three- and six-month periods. When his parents came to visit for six weeks, his former partner allowed them to see the kids for only two days.

Jeff has been prevented from getting any information from doctors and schools about the kids. The mother called the children's school to let them know that their father cannot have access to his children's information, and they accepted her instructions. She also asked the court on several occasions for a restraining order, which was granted each time. This resulted in serious difficulties for Jeff in his efforts to see his kids; criminal harassment charges were laid when he kept trying to see he kids, but these were eventually dropped.

Jeff states that he went through an extremely hard time emotionally for almost two years; he felt that everyone and everything was against him, including the courts and the B.C. government. Currently, he sees his children every Wednesday and every second weekend from Friday to Sunday. He still has a restraining order against him. He has no access to any of his children's school events, sports or extra-curricular activities.

## 41. Al

Al and his wife decided to separate after a lengthy period of marital problems. He left the family home to his wife and their three children, a three-year-old son, five-year-old son and nine-year-old daughter. This decision was made by mutual consent. In the beginning he had unlimited access to his kids. However, after legal proceedings started, access eroded, and he did not see the children for six months. He went back to court to change the access order. Access terms were changed with the mother's consent; she was not opposed to him seeing the children, but only at set times. He was allowed to see the children only every second weekend. When his oldest son turned sixteen, he moved in with Al. His younger son now also lives with him. The daughter stays with the mother, although she states that her mother will make her feel guilty if she goes to live with her father and brothers, which is her preference. However, Al now has good contact with her.

## 42. Michael

Michael's wife asked him to leave the house, which he did, reluctantly, after a ten-year marriage. In the beginning, he could see his boy, age eight, only sporadically. One of the reasons he lost contact with his son is that he did not respond to the legal papers, which he received on a day he was working (he is a professional stunt person). He had to respond to the documents within seventy-two hours. He states he did not read the papers because he was extremely busy on the set.

Michael indicates that he misses his child every day, but he does not like to talk about his pain and suffering. He has not seen his child in almost five years. He has had about twenty lawyers and spent $400,000 on legal fees. He believes that lawyers and judges are inherently corrupt and that the legal system should stay out of family issues.

Michael states that he has been a family man all his life; he comes from a large Catholic family where marriage and family responsibility are very important. Currently, he is fighting for custody of his child. However, he cannot find a lawyer who will take his case.

### 43. Jas

Jas's former partner took the children, a five-year-old son and four-year-old daughter, and moved away. The location was unknown to father. Police were not able to help him to locate the children. After he located his ex-wife and the children, there was constant access denial by mother. Access was always on the mother's terms; whatever she said he had to do. Now Jas has more regulation of access because of a court order and some compliance of the court order.

Jas states that there is a huge difference in parental lifestyles; the mother has a drinking problem while father is very health conscious. Currently he has non-custodial access; however, he has good contact with the kids.

### 44. David

David met his partner after she separated from her husband; she had been married for twenty years before the affair. After she gave birth to their son, now five years old, she started acting strangely. There were four episodes of psychotic behaviour (her own mother suffered from a lifelong depression disorder). He was interviewed by police for suspicion of domestic violence after she called 911, when he told his wife that he was going to push the door when she locked herself in the bathroom with their infant son.

Three weeks after that episode, he served her with an application for a provincial court order for custody. She replied by obtaining an ex parte order evicting him from the home and legally preventing him from being in contact with her or their son. As a result, he lost his home, savings and eventually his job. He hired a number of lawyers, who he states were worthless and dishonest. He considers the ex parte order to have been obtained by fraud.

David has not seen his son in three years. He believes that he is a victim of the gender bias of the court system. A psychologist wrote a parenting report that said that he was the one who had a psychiatric problem and that he has a narcissistic personality disorder, which he denies.

## 45. Richard

Richard separated from his wife when his daughters were four and two years old, leaving the marriage and the family home. In the beginning, he was able to see his children every two weeks. Richard signed an agreement (with the help of family justice counsellors recommended by his wife) which gave the mother legal sole custody. At that time, he was naïve about family law matters, whereas his wife was knowledgeable about the workings of the family justice system. He initially trusted his wife to guide them through the legal separation process; however, access difficulties began to surface, and then he lost access for almost two years. After two years, his ex-wife invited him to the house to see the girls. However, after almost a year his access again slowly decreased. He again went to family justice counsellors, who seemed helpful. He began to see, however, that he was being manipulated into signing away his legal rights by both his wife and the family justice counsellors.

According to Richard, the justice system is very complex and essentially a penal system. In particular, the courts and the Family Maintenance Enforcement Program have been extremely punitive to him.

Over the years, his daughters began to display serious acting-out behaviours related to their parents' conflict and the absence of their father in their lives. From the age of twelve (she is now fourteen), his older daughter has been experimenting with alcohol and dealing drugs, has been charged with shoplifting and theft, and has crashed her mother's car. As this daughter was out of her mother's control, she came to live with him. Currently, he is spending much more time with both his kids, the acting out of the older daughter has diminished, and his relationship with both his daughters is strong.

## 46. Robert

Robert divorced his wife when his daughter was thirteen months old. He went to court to establish his paternity as he and his wife had not been co-habiting prior to his daughter's birth. But the court refused his application and did not recognize any agreements that were previously made between the parties. Throughout the entire process, there were false allegations by his ex-wife of domestic violence and sexual abuse. His ex-wife alleged that he sexually abused his two-year-old daughter during access visits. He was investigated for six months; his child underwent the rape kit. The police never arrested him, and the allegations were found to be completely unfounded and made with malicious intent. The court ordered supervised access for him two days a week, three hours on Saturday and either Sunday or Monday. He estimates that the mother refused about 85 percent of the visits (365 out of 440 hours).

He has decided not to continue litigation. In his opinion, he wasted his time in the courts because of the gender-based discrimination of the B.C.

legal system. There is continual denial of fathers' rights by the court system. He has not seen his child for almost four years but is actively campaigning to reform the legal system and the child custody determination process.

## 47. John

John has four children, three daughters, twenty-four, twenty, and fourteen, and one son, who is twelve. His youngest daughter and son have resided with their mother since the separation, and his son is on medication to control seizures. He has been separated from his wife for five years, during which, he claims, his right to equal parenting responsibility has been violated by the legal system. He claims that the judicial system separated him from his children and abused him emotionally, treating him with disdain and disrespect. For example, he was arrested while he was trying see his children at home (his ex changed the locks after getting an ex parte order to do so); six police cars surrounded him, and he was taken away and has not been allowed back to the family home since, despite the fact that he ran his business from the family home. As a result, he has suffered serious physical and emotional problems requiring hospitalization.

John states that his former partner has made false allegations, denied access and engaged in parental alienation, all forms of child abuse, in his opinion. His kids has been severely negatively affected by the dispute. Currently, he is able to see the children once a week on Sunday.

## 48. Ray

Ray has two children, of which he is not the biological parent, as they were conceived by artificial insemination, but he adopted them. According to Ray, the children had been brainwashed against him for many years by his wife, in anticipation of separation. One day he was handed an ex parte order of a judgment that he knew nothing about; he had no knowledge or previous indication that this was going to occur. His legal counsel told him that if he waited one week he would have a better chance of his matter being heard. He waited one week; unfortunately, there was not enough time to hear his case. As a result, his case was dismissed, never heard. There were also charges laid against him of having assaulted his daughter. Until now, he still has no knowledge of the nature of the assault. He was given two options: go to jail while waiting for the matter to be heard, or sign an undertaking through a peace bond that he would not return to the family home. He signed the papers; no charges have ever been laid, but subsequent to the false allegation came a restraining order. He has not been allowed back home since that time.

He believes that his wife has been coached to undertake these actions by a local women's rights organization. Psychological assessments have been written in favour of restoring his relationship with his children; he has not been able, however, to obtain any legal redress on the matter. His relationship with his kids has been severely damaged; they are alienated and extremely hostile to him. He has not seen his children in two years.

### 49. Manfred
Manfred has two children, a daughter sixteen and a son twelve years old. He separated from his wife when the kids were seven and four because they had differences in parenting styles. Before they separation, they attended family counselling for one and a half years. According to Manfred, during the marriage, his ex-wife did not follow through with child behaviour management strategies or expectations, while he was doing everything he could, fixing the house and financially taking care of the family. He was not allowed to have any say in the parenting of the children, and as a result, he left the family.

In the beginning, he saw his kids often, with no fixed schedule. However, the situation has changed; he was threatened with not getting any time with his kids. He went to court but he was not satisfied with the results; there were no consequences for his ex-wife's denial of access. Currently he sees his kids once or twice a year.

### 50. Murray
Murray has four kids; three sons, now aged twenty-four, twenty-three and thirteen, and one daughter, age eleven. Just before separation, four years ago, Murray had been away in Calgary working for six weeks; after returning home, his partner asked him to leave and find his own place. He did leave, thinking that this would be only a short-term separation. His kids at first did not really understand why their father left or why their mom had a boyfriend. As time progressed, it became evident to Murray that the separation would be permanent, and it became more difficult for him to have access to his kids. He was rarely allowed to see them by his ex-wife. His ex-partner was told by a judge that the children should "see their dad as they are supposed to, or I will put you in jail." Currently, Murray's children visit him regularly.

### 51. Michael
Michael has two daughters, age eleven and eight. After he separated from his partner, he had a joint custody arrangement. In 2000, his ex-partner forged his signature on passport documents, allowing her to take the children out of the country. She went to Chile with the children without his knowledge. There was an ex parte order mailed to him from Chile. His ex-wife had accused him of sexual molestation of his daughters, which he denied. He was never charged. Since she kidnapped the children, he has lost almost all contact with his daughters. The last time he saw his children was one year ago for two hours, under supervision.

### 52. James

James has two daughters, now seventeen and thirteen, and one son, twelve years old. His marriage deteriorated in the last two years. He ended up in the hospital while his ex-wife announced to the children, "Daddy is not coming home; he does not want to live with us anymore." The kids came to believe that their father did not love them anymore. It took him some time and effort to change their perception about him.

Since that time, the divorce has become more amicable. Part of the divorce involved James coming out as a gay man. James never petitioned for custody but he has total access to his kids. He has a new male partner, and a very good relationship and contact with the children.

### 53. Steve

Steve was married for about five years, with no children, and had two separations in the middle of that time. When his son was only six weeks old, the mother took him and left the house. Steve did not know where his son was for almost a year. After that, his access was very limited, with unfounded allegations of spousal and child abuse. Later, he learned that he had married a survivor of incest. She decided to enter the day program at the local psychiatric hospital. During that time, Steve had his son almost 80 percent of the time and obtained a legally enforceable parenting order.

Numerous challenges followed, including conflicts with his son's school, involvement with child protective services and a period of supervised access, related to the ongoing conflict regarding parenting arrangements, after his ex-wife's discharge from the day program.

Eventually his ex-wife's threats regarding removing their son from his father's care subsided. Currently, he has joint custody, and his son's previous anxiety (related to fear of separation from his father) has stabilized. His relationship with his son (now thirteen years old) is excellent.

### 54. Raynor

Raynor separated in 2001. He states that during the marriage he spent a lot of time with his children. In the beginning of the separation, he had reasonable access to his three children, two girls, age twelve and eleven, and one son, age nine. Raynor then had some depressive episodes, and his access time was reduced.

Currently he sees his children twice a week. His relationship with the children is good. He feels that he cannot spend as much time with his children as he used to because he has to work to make money to be able to meet his financial support obligations.

## 55. Curtis

Curtis has four children, two boys, age eleven and eight, and two girls, age seventeen and fifteen. Prior to separation, his daughters revealed they were afraid of their mother. As more details about the mother's mental health problems and abusive behaviour toward all the children emerged, Curtis applied for sole custody of the four children. Upon learning of his intentions, his wife took the kids to a women's transition shelter. At the court hearing, false information provided by both mother and her lawyer were exposed, and the mother eventually admitted that her allegations of abuse against Curtis were false. The children disclosed that mother was lying to the workers in the transition house. Despite her lies in court, there were no consequences, and custody was granted to the mother. Curtis's relationship with his children began to deteriorate at that point; after several confrontations with court officials regarding lack of enforcement of access and a period of access supervision, Curtis' access time with his kids was reduced by the court.

Curtis maintains a bitter view of court officials and judges in particular. He claims that judges are not trained to deal with complex family matters, describes widespread corruption and has made formal complaints to the Law Society. He has concluded that the majority of judges are indifferent to the well being of children. He states that parental alienation, not just from one family member, but a whole extended family, should be made a crime in the Criminal Code. He has not seen his children in three years. His two eldest children have come to hate him because of brainwashing by their mother.

## 56. Thomas

Thomas and his family moved to Salt Spring Island from Vancouver, where they purchased a second house. After a while, his wife decided to return to their house in Vancouver, while he stayed behind, and that was the beginning of their problems. During one of his visits to Vancouver, his wife told him about her plans to separate. Upon returning to the island, he discovered that the house had been rented by his wife, and he had to find new accommodation. In the first year after separation, he had a hard time emotionally with visiting his children under numerous constraints, his daughters being seven and less than two years old at the time. For about five years, he would see the kids every second weekend. About five years later, in the midst of the court process, he received a fax from his oldest daughter (twelve at that time), stating that she wanted to have no part of him in her life. Since then he has had no contact with her, and his contact with his younger daughter has also declined. The court had ordered sole custody to the mother, access for the father and joint guardianship. He describes his ex-wife as extremely controlling and alienating, with access denial becoming routine, with police becoming involved on occasion. He describes the legal process as exacerbating conflict, first in relation to financial matters and then parenting. He also does not receive information about either of his children from their school; he believes that the mother has hindered his interactions with the teachers.

Currently, he has an ongoing relationship with the younger daughter but no relationship with either his older daughter or ex-wife. He remains extremely distraught about the process and outcome of his divorce.

### 57. Moray

Moray was working and completing his MA, while his wife was a stay-at-home mom. One day she asked him to move out of the house, which he refused to do. They sought counselling, while they continued to co-habit for a while. There was much fighting and mutual disrespect; she left the home and entered a women's transition shelter with the kids, alleging physical abuse. As a result, he moved out of the house. From that point, his former partner constantly kept the children away from him. He had very limited access. Her allegations of physical abuse were investigated, and he was cleared. There were two incidents of sexual abuse allegations against his roommate, and these were also cleared after a child protection investigation. However, Moray was denied access to his kids altogether (he supported his roommate through that time). In the next four years, he had twenty-two court appearances on the issue of custody and access, and he mainly represented himself, while his ex-wife had legal counsel. He obtained a court order for access, which was not honoured; he regrets having consented to sole maternal custody to end the protracted litigation. Moray has disengaged from his children's lives rather than subjecting them to continued acrimonious interaction. He has seen his kids only twice over the past four years.

### 58. Troy

Troy separated from his ex-wife in 2001; they had one daughter, age five. In the beginning, he had open and equal access to his child. After a BC Supreme Court order was made, his access was limited to every Wednesday and weekend. He went back to court and fought for equal time, but this resulted in further reduced access. Currently, he has access every second weekend and is reluctant to legally press the matter further. Despite his limited contact, his relationship with his daughter is good.

Troy indicates that he has always been very close to his daughter. He believes that children should have right to see each parent as they did before separation, the right not to be placed in a parental alienation position and the right to enjoy activities as they did before. They should be legal equal parenting time right off the bat, unless there is good reason otherwise.

### 59. Trevor

Trevor has five kids; the oldest daughter is adopted, age twenty-eight, a daughter age seventeen, son age fifteen, daughter age thirteen and son age eleven. His ex-wife wanted the divorce and sole custody; he moved out. He tried to negotiate with her lawyer, without any success. Finally, he went to court, where he received a joint custody arrangement. However, his parental time was manipulated; he got less than 39 percent of the time. He believes that the mother manipulated the legal process and used the children to obtain a favourable child support award.

However, Trevor's main interest is to be as actively involved as possible in raising his children. He strongly believes that both parents should be equally involved in raising their children. He believes that more dads should get actively involved in their children's lives, and fight for joint custody after separation. Currently, he has good contact with his children and their mom.

### 60. Chuck

Chuck had a very close relationship with his two daughters, now five and seven years old. After separation, Chuck had a bitter three-day trial, which resulted in guardianship and custody of the children being awarded to the mother. He was granted access of four hours every Sunday. According to Chuck, his former wife took advantage of women's advocates and a Canadian legal system biased against fathers. He feels that he was a victim of racial profiling by the judge, who assumed his peripheral involvement in his kids' lives as a legally unmarried African male (the couple were conjoined through a traditional religious ceremony in Nigeria).

Chuck wanted to limit direct contact with his ex-wife after the court process, and asked a Nigerian couple to pick up and drop off the kids on his behalf. The mother resisted this arrangement and denied access. About two years ago, she applied to the court to take the children to Nunavut for work reasons, and the court granted her request, despite the father's objections. In the end, she did not relocate.

He believes that the mother is taking advantage of the gender and racial bias of the Canadian family court system. He does not feel supported by courts or any government agencies. He believes that family courts in Canada are fundamentally unjust. Currently, Chuck does not have access to his kids, and hopes that they will seek him out when they are older.

### 61. Steve

Steve and his son's mother had one son, now age seventeen. For the first three years of his son's life, he was involved routinely as a daily caregiver, even though they never lived together (he was not working at the time). When Steve went back to work, the relationship dynamics changed, and the couple went to court. The BC Supreme Court increased his child support payments and gave him access of two weeknights and one Saturday per week, with no overnight visits, less than half of what he had before. When his son was three years old, he began wetting himself, and Steve was accused of sexual molestation of the boy. Investigation took place; he did the polygraph test, which he passed. Access was suspended during this time, and it took several months for police to drop the case with no charges. He had a long period of supervised visits with his son, and it took a long time to have this supervision removed.

After ten years of involvement with supervised access, psychologists, lawyers and judges, Steve gradually increased his contact and currently has a very good relationship with his son. His son's stated wishes to be with his father was the turning point in the lengthy process; his son now wants to live full-time with his father.

### 62. Lee

Lee's children, a girl and a boy, were three and seven at the time of separation. The parents both attended mediation to work out the differences between them. Lee left the home and paid child support. There were no court appearances. Lee's time with his children revolved around his work schedule (he is a musician). He made himself available as often as possible. Lee states that he did not feel fully supported as a father by the mother of his children, and this has created a barrier between him and the children. Currently, he has good relationship with his daughter; his relationship with his son is at arm's length.

### 63. Ken

Ken has twin sons, now age five. The parents separated during the pregnancy and he did not see his sons until they were eight months old. His lawyer did not apprise him about his rights, discouraged him and delayed action on the matter. He finally went to court, and was allowed see his sons three times a week for an hour, with the mother's brother supervising the visits. This "fishbowl" arrangement was supposed to be in effect for only four weeks, and that is why he reluctantly agreed to it, but it lasted much longer.

Eventually the matter was brought back to court and the access arrangement was changed and expanded. He was still dissatisfied with his lawyer and called a number of parenting support groups. He changed lawyers. Based on a parenting assessment, he received a significant increase in his court-ordered time with the children, starting with short frequent visits, which would expand to longer, less frequent visits. The mother, however, did not abide by the order. He called the police but they did not want to help. During that time he was collecting the needed paperwork to return to court. His ex-wife did everything she could to prevent her sons from having a relationship with their father, and he rarely saw the boys. His first overnight visit occurred two years after the court ordered overnight access.

He fired his second lawyer and decided to represent himself in court. He made a strong case for sole custody based on the mother's denial of access and his willingness to facilitate regular mother-child contact. In recognition that he was the more "friendly parent," Ken was awarded sole custody with generous access for the mother.

## 64. Phil

Phil and his wife had three children together. After the separation, they had a joint custody agreement, arranged between themselves, for about two years. After that time, he was served with papers for a court appearance for an application for sole custody for his ex-wife, which she was awarded. She had also chosen to move for the sake of her career.

After the court hearing, Phil's relationship with his children deteriorated rapidly, despite the fact that they'd had a very close relationship and had done many activities together. After the mother moved with the children, they were under her influence, and he had little input. Currently, he has a close relationship with his oldest and youngest sons. With his daughter, he keeps email contact. According to Phil, she is heartbroken because she feels that he somehow abandoned her.

## 65. Todd

Todd and his partner separated when their son was nine months old. The mother gained sole custody on an ex parte order. Father went to court sixty-nine times over five years to deal with access and enforcement of orders. In the meantime, his former partner moved with his child to Calgary, 400 miles away, against the court guardianship order. According to Todd, his ex-partner had serious drug addiction problems.

Todd obtained custody by default, when mother returned from Calgary and left their son with Todd. Although his son was now living with him, it took almost six months for the court to recognize paternal custody, even though child welfare authorities followed up, and along with the school system, acknowledged him as the custodial parent. Finally, a new judge granted legal sole custody to Todd. The mother has not seen her son in two years. She phoned five times for three birthdays and two Christmases, and sent five postcards.

## 66. Hugh

Hugh and his wife were married for about nine years. They had two children, one daughter, age twelve, and a son, age fourteen. After the birth of their second child, his wife started acting differently. She started getting violent, physically abusing him and the kids. Finally, he took the children and left the house. He obtained legal custody and had the children living with him full-time for one year.

When they went back to court, his ex-wife admitted to being violent, and the judge ordered her to get counselling; the counsellor recommended that she have supervised access. Very quickly, she had overnight visits each week. Currently, there is a shared custody agreement and the children live with each of their parents half the week.

### 67. Ron

Ron and his ex-partner had an amicable separation. They had four daughters together; the youngest was two and the oldest seven at the time of separation. They agreed to share the children between them. There was also a legal separation agreement on child support.

### 68. Steve

The parental separation occurred when his wife asked Steve to leave the family home. They had two sons, age five and nine at separation. After the separation, he was devastated for three months, living some distance away and visiting the kids. He then moved back to the neighborhood and had the kids half of the time. It was a very hard transition for him and for his older son. His son could not believe that mom and dad were not together; he thought that they had been a happy family. The younger son went with the flow. Steve still has a fifty/fifty custody arrangement. He is involved in all aspects of his sons' lives, and they have adjusted to the separation.

### 69. Avi

Avi and his ex-wife separated amicably, with an agreement to co-parent with equal time. At the time, their daughter was two years old. He remained very supportive and involved in his daughter's life. Two years later, his ex-wife decided that she wanted to have sole custody, as she wanted to relocate. She hired a lawyer who was very aggressive; according to Avi, she was a radical feminist lawyer. He felt that he was violated and misrepresented in the court. After a year and a half of acrimonious litigation, the judge upheld joint custody, joint guardianship and co-parenting. He spent $75,000 in legal fees; he had one of the best lawyers in town, whose gentle approach helped him a lot.

### 70. Robert

Just prior to separation, Robert was admitted to the hospital suffering from severe depression. He had attempted suicide as a response to his marital difficulties (abuse trauma) and work pressure. At the time, his children, both girls, were one and a half and three and a half (he is also the father of three boys from a previous marriage). He was served with divorce papers in the hospital ward. His wife used his mental breakdown as a mechanism to prevent him from having access to his children. Upon discharge, he was allowed to see the children for only a couple of hours each week. These visits took place while the divorce proceedings were going on and the court had not yet made an access order. He ended up having court-ordered access every other weekend, with no overnights. After that, he obtained an order allowing overnight access from Saturday afternoon to Sunday mornings, and eventually, over an eight-year period, court-ordered access increased to 42 percent time. However, his access has been continually obstructed by the mother and her allegations. Over the past eight years, he went to court ninety times to have access orders made and enforced. He has had to relocate to be with his children, after his wife moved from B.C. to Ontario and back. There have been numerous psychological assessments, and legal bills have left him financially destitute. All of this has taken a toll on his health. Currently he is remarried, has better access, and enjoys a good relationship with all of his children.

## 71. Roger

Roger was the primary caregiver for his son for the first seven months of his life. His wife then decided to move from B.C. to Ontario with their child. In Ontario she obtained an ex parte order for interim custody. For the first two weeks after the move, Roger did not hear from her and knew nothing of their whereabouts.

He flew to Toronto, where he went to court to fight for custody of his child. He wanted joint custody with residency with the mother and full access rights for the father. Roger's son would fly back home to his dad every summer; Roger would also have access to him other times of the year. Currently, his son is three years old and sees his dad twice a year (he flies out to see his dad).

There are ongoing issues; she wants daycare while she works and is thinking of going to university, and she wants him to pay the cost of the daycare. She is unwilling to consider sharing the cost of travel to see his child. He does not want to pay anything extra, as he already pays child support according to fixed guideline amounts.

## 72. David

David has three daughters, now age thirty, twenty-one and nineteen, and one son, age sixteen. During his marriage, he worked hard to financially support the family. He was very focused on his career; he was a ship's captain. His wife had an affair with his best friend, left with the kids and went to a women's transition shelter. The broken relationship with his children was a tremendous shock and loss; he suffered from so much pain that he could not concentrate. They went to court, he was evicted from the house and was granted supervised visits with his kids in the family home. He could see the children every week or every two weeks. His relationship with the children was difficult at the time. Currently his relationship with the children is good. He believes he is a better father now that he has worked through grieving the loss of the marriage and family. He received a lot of help from a support group, Fathers for Equality.

### 73. Harvey

Harvey separated when his two sons were twelve and seven. After they separated, the parents let the children decide with whom they were going to live. They stayed in the family home with their mother. The first couple of months were very stressful for Harvey. He found being away from the kids was very hard. He would see them two or three times a week. Currently he sees his children almost every weekend. They have a very good relationship.

### 74. Leford

Leford separated when his daughter was one year old. Before the final separation, the parents negotiated a custody agreement; he could see his daughter one week a month. His involvement in daughter's life was in fact very limited, however. He had to go to court to increase and enforce his access. The whole court process was a hellish experience for him; he realized that the court system is set up in favour of women. He experienced the court as having strong gender bias; there were no support groups available to him at that time.

It took three years for him to get regular access to his daughter. Currently, he spends two weeks with his child, then she goes to her mother for three weeks. According to Leford, child protection services were not supportive at all. He was twice told that they did not have the resources to investigate his complaints about the mother's abuse and mental health issues. The RCMP were also not helpful in regard to curbing the mother's threats and abusive behaviour. He believes that current child support guidelines promote the custodial parent denying access to the non-custodial parent.

### 75. Colin

Colin has three children, two girls, five and a half and three and a half, and one son, seven. About three years ago, Colin's wife acquired an ex parte order to have him removed from the family home. After they separated, he was able to see the children quite regularly. He rented a basement suite across the street. Almost a year after separation, his ex-wife demanded that his visits with the children be supervised, on the grounds that he was mentally unstable. (Colin subsequently suffered severe depression and he was out of work for almost six months). The mother tried to block him from seeing the children at all. Supervised access was ordered but eventually dropped after a psychological assessment/custody and access evaluation supported increased access for Colin. The divorce trial will start soon. Currently, he is living in co-op housing and sees the kids two nights a week. His children desperately want to spend more time with their dad.

## 76. Randy

Before Randy separated, he was a stay-at-home parent. He had a lot of time with his kids, as he worked as a school bus driver. He has four children, three sons, now age twenty, eighteen and twelve, and one daughter, age ten. After they separated, the parents agreed on a shared parenting schedule (weekly rotations) for the kids. Eventually, the mother decided that she did not want to continue the schedule, and that was the beginning of the custody battle. She refused to allow him to see the kids, finding various excuses. He tried to go to court a couple of times to get access enforced but without success, although at that time, they had legal joint custody.

When he continued to try to enforce the joint custody order, his ex-wife accused him of molesting his daughter (she was three at the time). Three doctors examined his daughter; no evidence was ever found. When they went to court, the mother insisted on supervised access for the father. He ended up doing supervised visitations for about four months. Eventually the supervision was dropped, but by that time the mother had obtained legal sole custody, which the court was reluctant to change.

A month before the custody and access hearing, the mother moved the kids from Victoria to Nanaimo. The judge stated she should not have moved the children without permission and ordered her to bring them back. According to Randy, the judge also suggested that she should make an application to keep the kids in Nanaimo, which she did, successfully. Currently, he tries his best to see the kids as an access parent, on a long distance basis, every second week. Distance and his work schedule do not allow him see the kids every week.

## 77. Dave

Dave's wife had an affair; she took their five-year-old daughter and left him, moving from Whistler to Victoria. In the beginning, they had a shared parenting arrangement; his daughter stayed with each parent an equal amount of time. When he moved to Victoria, his former partner started to renege on the plan. Eventually, she said she wanted Dave out of their lives altogether. There were periods when he did not see his child for three or four weeks.

After attending court, the parents decided on a collaborative law approach. Their lawyers decided that they could not do much more for them and suggested they seek out a divorce coach.

Currently, they see a psychologist (for divorce coaching) twice a week for two-hour sessions. They have a strict access agenda to follow. Since they started seeing the psychologist, Dave's contact with the kids has been restored. They remain at an impasse, however, on the issue of parenting. Dave believes that shared parenting is in their daughter's best interest; the mother has stepped back and wants sole residential custody.

## 78. Bill

Bill and his former partner had an amicable separation; they wanted to make it as easy as possible for the kids, two daughters age twenty-seven and twenty-four, and one son, age seventeen. He wanted the children to live with him, and the mother consented to this arrangement. The younger two children moved in with him; the oldest had already left home.

## 79. Mike

Mike has one daughter, age twelve. He left the family home because he found that there was too much emotional stress. When he left, he did not see his daughter for almost a year. After he went to court, he was able see his daughter initially for two hours a week, to be increased over time. According to Mike, the court process was very emotionally draining, and many things were said that were not true. The mother made him look like an evil person, accusing him of hard drug abuse. He had to submit to drug testing and get letters from his employer, doctor and family members, which helped in the end.

Currently he is not seeing his daughter. He is supposed to see her after school every Friday from 4 p.m. and take her to school at 9 a.m. Monday. However, his ex-wife does not abide by the order. He does not know where his daughter lives or what school she attends.

## 80. Alan

Alan had two daughters, age six and nine at the time of his divorce in 1968. The couple divorced because of her infidelity. After they divorced, he stayed in the family home for three months until they had a separation agreement. He was awarded "liberal access" to the children without any specified days or hours. In his opinion, this was his biggest error because access was left to the interpretation of the individuals involved, and in this case his wife had custody. As a result, for the next ten years, he had to fight to see his children. He saw his younger child on a very restricted basis. He went back to court and ended up getting access for one day each month.

In the beginning, he had a very good relationship with his daughters. He has since lost contact with his older daughter, who allied herself with her mother. He is closer to his younger daughter. The children are now adults; he has four grandsons.

## 81. Arnie

Arnie characterized his former partner as constantly irrational and hysterical, and as a result, he left the family home. He lived in his car and cabin for a while after the separation. The mother's behaviour would trigger emotional "freezing" in the children. Arnie was alienated from his children, two girls, age thirteen and nine, and one son, age eleven. The mother would simply not show up with the children when he was scheduled for access visits. She would act hysterically in front of the children, claiming that her distress was the father's fault. Arnie's extended family has also been alienated from the children. His showing up at the children's events (such as soccer) is stressful for all involved. Currently, his relationship with children is threatened and falling apart. Arnie recently bicycled across Canada in an attempt to draw public attention to the plight of divorced fathers.

### 82. Grant

Grant and his ex-partner have one daughter, age three at separation. The couple had many difficulties throughout their marriage, including different ideas and cultural practices regarding parenting, with the mother adopting a more controlling and punitive approach toward their daughter. There were numerous arguments that resulted in the mother verbally and sometimes physically attacking Grant. At the same time, the mother threatened Grant with calling the police, which she did, and he was once removed from the home, with no charges laid. He returned to live at home, and a year later police were again called by his wife, and this time he was charged and went to jail for the night. When he went back to the house, the mother and daughter were gone. He has not seen his daughter or ex-partner since that incident three years ago.

All his requests to see his daughter have been denied. Court has been a drawn-out process, with the access problem left unresolved as the criminal matter has been left in abeyance. Currently his former partner and daughter are in Iran. The court process continues.

# Chapter 4

# Children's Needs and Paternal and Social Institutional Responsibilities

## Pre- and Post-Divorce Father-Child Relationships

As is evident from fathers' accounts of their divorce experiences, most of the fathers who volunteered for the study were non-custodial or non-residential fathers, and many of these had lost contact with their children. In fact, sixty-five of the eighty-two fathers were non-custodial fathers, and thirty of these men were disengaged from their children's lives, not having had contact with their children over the past six months. Table 4-1 contains the breakdown of the actual living arrangements of the fathers we interviewed and their legal custody designations.

In regard to actual living arrangements with children, there were sixty-five non-custodial fathers, eleven in joint custody arrangements and six with sole (paternal) custody; of the sixty-five non-custodial fathers, fifty-six were involuntary non-custodial fathers. Although only eleven dads had joint custody in reality, twenty-seven had legal joint custody designations. Thus, it seems that courts are designating physical sole maternal custody arrangements as "joint custody." The discrepancy between legal designations

*Table 4-1 Legal Custody Designations versus De Facto Living Arrangements*

Fathers' actual living arrangements with children
    Non-custodial (less than 40% time): 65
        58 involuntary; 7 voluntary
        30 disengaged
    Joint custodial (40–60% time): 11
    Sole custodial (more than 60% time): 6

Fathers' legal custody designations
    Non-custodial access: 22
    Joint custodial: 27
    Sole custodial: 7
    Other (no order; no contact order): 22
    NA or missing: 4

and actual living arrangements is striking. This finding flies in the face of legal commentators who insist that courts are now routinely awarding joint physical custody; courts do award joint custody, but it is joint custody in name only.

One of the most significant findings of the study was that a marked discontinuity exists between pre- and post-divorce parent-child living arrangements, more marked than in my earlier study, in the direction of equal or shared parenting before divorce shifting to sole maternal custody after divorce (see Table 4-2). Whereas thirty-eight of eighty-two fathers reported shared parenting arrangements before divorce (defined as 40 percent or more of a child's time spent with each parent), only eleven fathers reported shared parenting arrangements after divorce. Whereas twenty of eighty-two fathers reported primary maternal care arrangements before divorce, sixty-five reported primary maternal care arrangements after divorce. These findings stand in marked contrast to what fathers say they want in regard to post-divorce living arrangements with their children. The most beneficial living arrangement for children, according to sixty-nine of the fathers, is equal or shared parenting. When asked what legal child custody presumption should be in place, sixty-four fathers (78 percent) identified equal or shared parenting. This is consistent with public opinion polls; a recent Canadian government survey (N=1,002) obtained almost 80 percent public support for

*Table 4-2 Discontinuity between Pre- and Post-Divorce Father-Child Relationships and Paternal Preferences*

Discontinuity between pre- and post-divorce father-child relationships

|  | Pre- | Post- |
|---|---|---|
| Primary paternal care | 18 | 7 |
| Primary maternal care | 20 | 64 |
| Equal / shared | 38 | 11 |
| Other | 6 | - |

What fathers want post-divorce

|  | BIOC* | Legal |
|---|---|---|
| Primary paternal care | 4 | - |
| Primary maternal care | 4 | 2 |
| Equal / shared | 69 | 64 |
| Other | 5 | 12 |
| Approximation Standard | - | 4 |

* Best interests of the child

federal and provincial legislation to create a presumption of equal parenting in child custody cases, with almost no difference by gender (78.3 percent of women and 77.7 percent of men were in support).

When I compared my research findings with those I obtained in my study twenty years ago, I found that the outcomes for fathers and their children have considerably worsened, despite the fact that fathers are taking a much more active role in child care before divorce today than they did twenty years ago. In 1989 (published in *Divorce and Disengagement* in 1993), I found a discontinuity between pre- and post-divorce parenting patterns, with previously highly involved and attached fathers more likely to lose contact with children after divorce than those who reported being previously less involved and attached. I found that a strong pre-divorce father-child attachment bond predisposes fathers to deeper feelings of loss and a pronounced grief reaction after divorce. The present study found an even greater discontinuity between pre- and post-divorce living arrangements, in the direction of equal or shared parenting before divorce shifting to primary maternal custody after divorce. Table 4-3 compares the findings of my 1989 and 2010 studies.

In 1989 I found that while twenty-eight of forty "contact" fathers (those

*Table 4-3 Pre- vs. Post-Divorce Father-Child Relationships (1989 & 2010 Studies)*

Discontinuity between pre- and post-divorce father-child relationships (fatherhood involvement, attachment and influence) (Kruk 1989)

| Pre-Divorce Relationship | Post-Divorce Contact | |
| --- | --- | --- |
| | Contact | Disengagement |
| Low Involvement, Attachment & Influence | 28 | 14 |
| High Involvement, Attachment & Influence | 12 | 26 |
| TOTAL | 40 | 40 |

Discontinuity between pre- and post-divorce father-child relationships (fatherhood involvement) (Kruk 2010a)

| | Pre-Divorce | Post-Divorce |
| --- | --- | --- |
| Primary Paternal Care | 18 | 6 |
| Primary Maternal Care | 20 | 65 |
| Equal / Shared | 38 | 11 |
| Other | 6 | - |
| TOTAL | 82 | 82 |

who maintained regular contact with their children after divorce) reported low levels of pre-divorce involvement, attachment and influence, and better adaptation to the consequences of divorce, twenty-six of forty disengaged (no contact) fathers had comparatively high scores on all indices relating to the pre-divorce father-child relationship and marked problems in post-divorce adaptation. In the present study, whereas thirty-eight of eighty-two fathers reported shared parenting arrangements before divorce, only eleven reported shared parenting arrangements after divorce. Whereas twenty fathers reported primary maternal care arrangements before divorce, sixty-five reported primary maternal care arrangements after divorce, with thirty of these fathers disengaged from their children's lives. It appears that more fathers are now engaged in shared parenting in two-parent families, yet relatively more fathers are becoming disengaged when removed as primary or co-caregivers after divorce.

In 1989, I also found a marked discrepancy between what fathers desired in regard to their post-divorce living arrangements with their children and final outcomes. Seventy-nine percent of fathers reported that they wanted their children to live with them at least part of the time. Fathers held the discouragement of legal practitioners and a legal child custody system that they perceived to be biased against fathers as the reason why they were unable to obtain what they desired. In the present study, fathers expressed an even stronger preference for a shared parenting arrangement after divorce; sixty-nine fathers (84 percent) identified equal or shared parenting as in the best interests of their children. When asked what legal presumption should be in effect when parents are in dispute over post-divorce parenting arrangements, sixty-four fathers (78 percent) indicated equal or shared parenting.

## The Fathers' Narratives

The more in-depth questions in my study asked fathers to recount the story of their divorce and their views of children's needs, their responsibilities as fathers and the responsibilities of social institutions to support fathers during and after divorce.

The synopses in Chapter 3 are accurate summaries of fathers' more detailed storied accounts. The members of the research team independently summarized the fathers' narratives of their divorce experiences, and these summaries were collated and compared. In each case there was agreement regarding the salient features of the stories. We now turn to a more detailed analysis of fathers' accounts of their divorce experiences.

As is evident from their narratives, fathers painted a bleak picture of life after divorce, one of forced estrangement from children's lives. For most, these were stories of broken and, in some cases, restored attachments. Table 4-4 summarizes the core elements of the fathers' narrative accounts.

*Table 4-4 Narrative Storytelling: Themes and Story Pattern*

| Core Themes | Story Patterns |
|---|---|
| 1. Grief and loss; broken attachments with children | 1. Precipitating event; family stress, tension |
| 2. Mothers' discouragement of contact, access denial, and parental alienation; mothers as gatekeepers; importance of mothers' encouragement of contact | 2. Lack of external social support |
| | 3. Mothers as initiators of separation and divorce |
| | 4. Financial dispute leading to child custody dispute; legal system involvement |
| 3. Adversarial system heightening conflict; support services non-existent or unhelpful | 5. Parental alienation; abuse allegations |
| 4. Conflict and violence; abuse of fathers, especially legal abuse: sole custody/removal of custody; false allegations | 6. Heightened conflict; violence; initial paternal disengagement |
| | 7. Effects of conflict and paternal disengagement on children |
| 5. Effects on children: children's needs not being met; fear and worry regarding children's (emotional) well-being | 8. Structural and psychological obstacles to father-child involvement and attachment |
| 6. Financial losses | 9. Involuntary paternal disengagement; legal removal of custody |
| 7. Positive outcomes: father-child involvement and attachment | 10. Attempts to reestablish relationship; fathers as self-litigants |
| 8. Other themes: new relationships: new partners, remarriage and birth of children; relocation of custodial mother; lack of adequate legal representation | |

Eight core themes emerged from fathers' narrative accounts of their divorce process, particularly in regard to their relationship with their children.

1. *Grief and loss; broken attachments with children.* Divorced fathers experience a grieving process that contains all the major elements of bereavement, primarily linked to the loss of their children and the weakening of the father-child attachment bond. Although many fathers continued to have contact with their children, the quality of the attachment bond suffered as a result of diminished time in the daily routines of the relationship; routine access to and engagement with children was seen as a prerequisite

of paternal attachment to and responsibility for children. The threatened loss of the father-child relationship was present even for custodial fathers. The importance of sufficient time, financial security, autonomy and equality in parenting were identified by fathers as critical in preserving meaningful attachments with their children.

> Painful, painful is the operative word, and mind-blowingly awful, disgusting, disheartening, grief. (Curtis, participant 55)

> I made constant attempts to see the children, and she just completely thwarted it, and I ended up in the psych ward for two months, and then I was a vegetable, I was a complete emotional vegetable, and I actually went home to Nova Scotia and was off work, obviously... I said to the cops, here's the deal. I've had it with this, I'm going to be standing in front of this house for the next ninety-six hours waiting for my kids, so they said they didn't really want me to do that, so I just went home got a placard and I wrote on it, "waiting for my children as ordered by the supreme court." (Hal, 25)

> I thought everything was going to end, the pain in my head was excruciating. There was so much pain. I had never experienced that pain before. I tried going to work but I couldn't even concentrate. (David, 72)

2. *Mothers' discouragement of contact, access denial and parental alienation; mothers as gatekeepers; importance of mothers' encouragement of contact.* The central importance of mothers' gatekeeping role and encouragement for the maintenance of the father-child relationship was a second core theme. In some cases, fathers were able to preserve their attachments with their children after divorce; in many others, however, mothers' discouragement of paternal involvement was associated with paternal disengagement. The vulnerable nature of father-child attachments was noted by the majority of fathers, and access denial and parental alienation were core features of many fathers' stories.

> She was telling them that if I went and picked them up or whatever, they'd never see her, or granny, or auntie again, that I was going to kidnap them. (Joe, 1)

> I learned subsequently she'd been telling the children for over a year that daddy's bad, daddy can't be trusted, to that effect. Mommy loves you. Daddy doesn't love you... She's still controlling, whenever we're planning something, if it doesn't suit her, she won't let him come over, has some excuse. That he has chores to do, if he doesn't do his chores then he can't go see daddy. (John, 4)

> Access was completely denied, even though there was a court order for me to spend time with him. So it was awful, getting out the gate.

> Things have been awful ever since then, and to cut to today, after seven years, our court order is constantly being defied. (Preston, 7)

3.   *Adversarial system heightening conflict; support services non-existent or unhelpful.* Fathers' narratives focused on the role of the adversarial system in heightening conflict and fueling family violence, especially when parent-child attachment bonds were threatened. At the same time, fathers were forced to rely on non-professional mutual aid or self-help groups for support, and few fathers availed themselves of these services. Professional support services for divorced fathers were either not available or unhelpful, as they did not address fathers' stated needs.

> I went to court sixty-nine times during five and a half years to deal with access issues and enforcement of orders. And then my ex moved with the child to Calgary, 400 miles away against court ordered guardianship. (Todd, 65)

> Nothing ever happens to her. She just basically goes along and does whatever she wants and nothing ever happens to her... She denies access for a month and I actually got to the point where I went to the police and I said I want to lay a charge and they're like, we don't deal with this; it's a civil matter. (Hal, 25)

> He (the judge) thought I had delusions of grandeur, because I wanted so strongly to have regular access to my child... He granted the mother sole custody. He wrote these three sentences, number one, the father has a basic misunderstanding of the role of the father in a child's life, number two, the mother believes that joint custody can never work for any child even if both parents are fully cooperative and fully communicative. This attitude of the mother's, he wrote, is very unhealthy for the child. And thirdly, he wrote, with this order for sole custody to the mother the father fears, with good reason, that the paternal relationship will be choked off entirely. And yet they're supposed to act in the paramount best interest of the child and it's in the best interest of the child to have all of their relationships choked off on the paternal side. (Alan, 33)

4.   *Conflict and violence; abuse of fathers, especially legal abuse: sole custody/ removal of custody; false allegations.* Spousal abuse was reported by several fathers, including physical, emotional and (especially) legal abuse (police involvement, false allegations, criminal charges, unsubstantiated allegations, sole custody and restraining orders). Fathers also described severe stress symptoms and the development of physical and mental health problems associated with legal proceedings. In some cases, false allegations put fathers on the defensive in the legal process; much time and financial resources were spent in countering allegations. When

allegations were not substantiated, fathers' attachments to their children had already been broken, and the legal system failed to restore father-child contact.

> My lawyer said it was a waste of time to try to get custody of the kids or even have joint custody. You two do not agree, therefore the judge will not provide joint custody... It is quite likely that the longer the alienation stands the greater are the chances of irreparable damages to the kids. (Thomas, 56)

> I had done a little bit of research at the UBC law library and I realized I was in a losing battle here and fathers have no rights and I kind of saw it coming after about three or four years of being beat up... I saw the best lawyers, any lawyers that I could talk to, they all said the same thing, that I had no rights, no say, and that was the law and sorry about your luck basically. (Darrell, 29)

> Throughout the entire court process it was allegations of domestic violence, sexual abuse, everything, I've had it all thrown at me in attempt to thwart my relationship with my child... The allegations were found to be completely unfounded and made with malicious intent, and this malicious intent has further hampered my parental time with my child. But it didn't do me any good in court, bringing all that material forward to a judge. Put it this way, it all got swept under the table. (Rob, 46)

5. *Effects on children: children's needs not being met; fear and worry regarding children's (emotional) well being.* Fathers' stories focused on the effects of divorce and ruptured father-child attachment bonds on their children. Children's well being, according to fathers, largely depends on fathers' active involvement in their lives in a parental capacity and not in a "visiting" context. Father-child attachment was defined in terms of responsibility-to-needs, that is, children were seen to need responsible father involvement in their lives in order to have their basic needs met, particularly emotional and attachment needs.

> My son had an absolute temper tantrum when they found out that they couldn't see me... It was obvious that she was sharing all the aspects of our disagreements with them and at that point, my son became more and more angry, withdrawn, confused, hostile, difficult to control, temper tantrums, really hard to control at times. (Theo, 18)

> To alienate a child, not just from one family member, but from a whole side of their family, should be in the Criminal Code. (Curtis, 55)

> I would rather never see my kids than go back through what I and the kids went through. (Moray, 57)

6. *Financial losses.* The enormous financial losses incurred by fathers,

resulting from both legal fees and child support payments, was the sixth theme. Debt and bankruptcy resulting from legal costs was a concern of most fathers. Loss of house and home, loss of children's inheritance, financial pressure imposed by the court and child support being defined strictly in financial terms were reported.

> I was told that even though I had it in writing, I had to go back to the court, spend more money, and petition the court to have my wife charged with contempt. I didn't have the emotional strength left. Fifty-five thousand dollars at that point and I still don't have a relationship with my daughters. (John, 4)

> So now we'd gone from living — our home in Calgary is now worth $380,000 — so I'd gone from making $70,000 a year, living in an exclusive neighbourhood, to living in a town, working in a call centre, and now I was living in a trailer. (Paul, 12)

> I've spent $275,000, all my RRSPs, the equity I had in my house, as much as I hate to say it, my son's education fund, my parent's retirement fund, they helped me to the tune of $100,000. Just to get to where we're at today, and all I really wanted was to be involved and to have a say. (Jim, 26)

7.  *Positive outcomes: father-child involvement and attachment.* Those fathers who were able to surmount the many obstacles to restoring their relationship with their children focused on positive outcomes and restoration of father-child bonds. All fathers valued their attachment to their children and saw their paternal role as central to their lives, and this was evident in virtually all the fathers' stories.

> Her mom encourages her to come to me and stuff like that, so it is getting better. (Jamie, 34)

> I strongly feel the main reason why I got custody of my boys is because I am the parent that is more willing to nurture the boys' relationship with the other parent. (Ken, 63)

> My daughter was two years old and the mom recognized that I was as important if not more important in meeting our daughter's needs ever since she was born… I was supportive and involved. (Avi, 69)

8.  *Other themes.* Finally, other themes in fathers' stories of diminished attachments to their children were noted: new partner and child responsibilities were associated with disengagement of fathers from children; relocation of custodial mothers was associated with disengagement of fathers from children; and lack of adequate legal representation (as a result of cost, difficulty of case and level of

disagreement and conflict) was widely reported. The slow pace of legal processes (dependent on lawyers' schedules), the use of ex parte orders and questionable legal advice (in regard to maternal relocation with children, rights of unmarried fathers who are separated before the birth of child and repercussions of the status quo with legal delays) were cited

The ten core elements that emerged from fathers' storied accounts of their divorce experiences and their diminished relationships with their children followed a certain progression. Fathers described a process where attachment stability was replaced by chaos in the father-child relationship. The following story elements are combined as a continuous narrative:

1.  *Precipitating event; family stress, tension.* Fathers' stories typically started with a precipitating stressful event, leading to family turmoil, with few social supports available. Examples included medical crisis (cancer, death of a child), loss of employment, infidelity and coming out. For some, the precipitating crisis was the separation itself, the former partner's new relationship or the father's new relationship. For some, the precipitating crisis was the legal decree itself.

2.  *Lack of external social support.* Fathers identified a lack of responsibility on the part of representatives of social institutions, including courts, child welfare agencies and the school system. Many fathers sought support but could not find it; others found services unhelpful. Court involvement was reported as exacerbating conflict.

3.  *Mothers as initiators of separation and divorce.* Fathers described the reaction of their partners to the precipitating event. Most fathers were respondents and mothers initiators of the divorce. Fathers gave up or kept going to court in an effort to preserve their relationship with their children. Some eventually had successful outcomes, obtaining joint custody orders, although mothers continued to breach access orders without consequence.

4.  *Financial dispute leading to child custody dispute; legal system involvement.* Conflict between the couple was reported by fathers as initially financially based; what started out as a financial disagreement later involved children as "bargaining chips." Because child custody has implications for child support, child custody became an issue of disagreement and conflict between the couple.

5.  *Parental alienation; abuse allegations.* Parental alienation occurred in degrees, as follows: no facilitation or encouragement of paternal contact; no consultation and unilateral decision-making by mothers regarding children; abuse allegations; and direct parental alienation. Early threats to remove the father as a custodial parent, which has profound repercussions

for parent-child attachment, was seen by fathers as a precursor of parental alienation.

6.  *Heightened conflict; violence; initial paternal disengagement.* Initial father disengagement occurred when conflict between parents escalated, or when either the mother or father was violent; police involvement was present in some cases.

7.  *Effects of conflict and paternal disengagement on children.* The effects of paternal disengagement on children then became manifest. Children witnessing conflict were seen by fathers to be at heightened risk, as their need for safety, order and stability were compromised. Behavioural problems among boys was a frequent result of witnessing parental conflict.

8.  *Structural and psychological obstacles to father-child involvement and attachment.* Both psychological and structural barriers mitigated against fathers in their efforts to restore their involvement with and attachment to their children. Structural obstacles to the father-child relationship included the lack of effective support services and adversarial legal processes; psychological obstacles to the father-child relationship were described as the result of power struggles between parents. When conflict occurred during transitions from one home to the other, children's loyalties become divided, and several fathers disengaged from their children's lives at that point.

9.  *Involuntary paternal disengagement; legal removal of custody.* Fathers disengaged when social institutions undermined their status as parents and imposed restrictions on the father-child relationship, including limited access, supervised access and lack of access to medical or school information. Young children were at the highest risk of paternal disengagement.

10.  *Attempts to re-establish relationship; fathers as self-litigants.* Fathers went to great lengths to re-establish a relationship with their children, and sometimes their persistence yielded positive results. In other cases, however, serious physical and mental health problems became manifest — a reflection of the strength of father-child attachment bonds before divorce.

What struck me the most from fathers' accounts is how much worse things are for those fathers who are involved in a custody dispute than they were twenty years ago. Whereas twenty years ago fathers were reporting a grief reaction over the loss of their children, today they are manifesting clear symptoms of full-blown post-traumatic stress.

## Children's Needs, Paternal Obligations and Social Institutional Responsibilities

The primary focus of my study was fathers' views of their children's needs in the divorce process, as fathers, along with mothers, are the real "experts" in regard to the "best interests" of their children. Their views on this most contentious question in the child custody arena have been unexamined to this point.

My study revealed one key finding previously unreported in the father involvement literature: divorced fathers view the "best interests" of their children in terms of their children's needs, defined as the nutriments or conditions essential to a child's growth and integrity. These needs may be roughly divided into physical and "metaphysical" needs. Both are important, as in some cases physical needs were emphasized by fathers, but in most cases children's emotional, psychological, social, moral and spiritual needs were seen to be of paramount importance.

According to fathers, children's social, emotional, psychological, moral and spiritual needs are not being addressed during and after divorce, much to children's detriment.

> They need emotional stability, they need love, obviously, they need to know that both parents care for them. (David, 15)

In order for these needs to be met, children require, first and foremost, a stable and unthreatened parental (not "access" or visiting) relationship with both their fathers and their mothers ("shared parenting"; "children need both parents").

> Children should be put in the position where they view their parents equally and that they see that everyone else views their parents equally, and that there is not a preferred parent… They have the need to believe that they still have two parents that each parent is as important as the other and that they are as important as they were before. (Hal, 25)

> I think it's very simple. They need the ongoing love, and affection, and attention, and guidance, and support, and nurturing, from both parents equally. And it's my belief that that's what gives them the highest degree of security and stability in their life. (Brad, 5)

Children need to be loved and in no way to feel to blame for their parents' divorce.

> They need to know that mom and dad still love them, that they're not part of the problem, that it's not their fault, and they need to be able to have access to both parents. (Joe, 1)

> I believe children need to know that they are loved by both parents and they need to be assured that the troubles are not anything to do with them. (Craig, 10)

> I think they need reassurance that it's not their fault. That it's got nothing to do with them, that they're not responsible. I think they need to be loved. Pure and simple. I think they need to be kept out of the issues

> between the parents. I think they need to know that it's okay for them
> to have a relationship with both their parents. (Theo, 18)

Children need a sense of security, safety and protection in often traumatizing situations.

> They need to have a sense of security, and that can only come by a
> well-thought-out, planned separation. That's pretty critical because if
> you give them a sense of how to resolve conflict and to realize that
> by cooperating, and no matter what mutually accepted conclusion,
> that can be peaceful. You can still have differences with people, but
> there doesn't need to be a toe-to-toe, nose-to-nose battle. I think that
> probably would be the crux of it, having that sense of security...First
> and foremost is protection from harm. (John, 4)

> To know that they're safe and that both parents are equal and care for
> them. (David, 2)

Parental cooperation and respect were also core themes discussed by fathers.

> They need something that will minimize the conflict between the
> parents. (Hal, 25)

> Children need to see that both parents have input into their lives...
> They need to see that the parents can discuss and communicate
> effectively. (Wren, 27)

> They need parents to be civil to each other with no vindictiveness and
> no turmoil. (Bob, 35)

> A relationship with both parents which is free of any negative situations.
> That they not be subjected to any discord between the parents, if there
> is any. (Steve, 61)

Children's needs for stability and consistency in their routines and relationships were also highlighted.

> Any separation from the nurturing routines provided in parental roles
> by either parent is likely to be traumatic for the child or produce some
> sort of effect. (Roger, 71)

> To try and keep your relationship as normal as possible and to reassure
> them of your love and no mater what happens that you will always be
> their father and that you will always be there for them. (Murray, 50)

> They need to have some stability, emotional stability, I guess, is
> important. Some consistency in decision-making and whatnot, so that
> they can learn by that. (Bruce, 3)

Interestingly, a significant number of fathers identified the need for family and cultural roots as central to children's well being, and under threat when they are cut off from their fathers and extended family.

> There has to be a mandated presumption of shared parenting responsibilities where both parents have a meaningful, consistent, stable ability to have their relationship with their children established to continue... Children should have a meaningful ability to access their extended family members, grandparents and other extended family members of both parents... Anything that undermines the ability to co-parent is against the best interests of the child. (Avi, 69)

Fathers were asked to identify all of their children's needs in the divorce transition, in order of importance. Fathers were highly variable in regard to the number of needs they identified. Table 4-5 lists, first, which need fathers reported to being their children's most important need, then which needs were reported among their children's top three needs, and then the sum total of all needs identified. Most important to note is that despite the judicial system's primary concern about fathers' child support obligations in regard to children's financial needs, fathers consider their children's unmet emotional needs as more important than their physical (including financial support) needs. Further, rather than focusing on children's need for their father in particular, fathers referred to the primary importance of children

| *Table 4-5 Needs of Children after Parental Divorce* | | | |
|---|---|---|---|
| | Most Important Need | Top 3 Needs | Total No. Fathers Identifying |
| Shared parenting | 26 | 45 | 66 |
| Stable relationship with both parents | | | |
| Love | 23 | 40 | 48 |
| Reassurance that children are not to blame | | | |
| Safety, Security | 13 | 52 | 59 |
| Physical needs: food, shelter, clothing | 8 | 24 | 73 |
| Financial provision | | | |
| Roots | 3 | 10 | 40 |
| Parental cooperation | 2 | 12 | 25 |
| Mutual respect | | | |
| Stability, Consistency | -- | -- | 25 |

having two active and responsible parents, of having a mom and a dad, and having ample time with both parents. This above all was identified by fathers as children's primary need in the divorce transition: the active and responsible involvement of both parents in children's lives, in a routine parental capacity as opposed to a "visiting" role. And children's other needs, particularly the need for reassurance that their parents still loved them and that the children were not to feel to blame for the divorce, and children's needs for safety and security, were connected to the primary need for a stable and unthreatened relationship with both parents after divorce.

Fathers viewed their children's "best interests" through the lens of what they could provide relation to their children's unmet needs. Fathers were then asked to identify their paternal responsibilities in relation to their children's needs. Again, fathers were highly variable in regard to the number of paternal responsibilities they identified. Table 4-6 lists, first, which paternal responsibility fathers reported to be the most important to children in the divorce transition, then which responsibilities were reported as among fathers' three most important responsibilities, and then the sum total of all paternal responsibilities identified. When asked about paternal responsibilities to children in the divorce transition, most fathers cited the responsibility to physically "be there" for their children, in a loving parental capacity.

> The responsibilities of the divorced father is to be there emotionally for their son or daughter and to be there to support them and let them know that they will always be there for them and that they'll always love them. (Craig, 10)

> I would say the main responsibility is to maintain contact, maintain a relationship. Maintain a sense of security and love that they would have felt in the family unit to the best of their abilities. (Theo, 18)

> Hang in there through thick and thin; maintain your same position in terms of your goal as a parent as opposed to the quote, "Disneyland Dad."... Maintain your parental role. (Hal, 25)

> To be a positive role model and to show through example the strength and the love they will need to go through life. (Jim, 26)

This was followed closely by the notion that fathers basically have only one responsibility — respect for their children's needs — which reflects the idea that children's best interests are commensurate with their basic needs.

> Make sure their needs are met, regardless of anything. Let the child know you love them, whenever you can. (Alan, 33)

> Maintain contact, be there, put the child's needs before own, make them feel like a person, show them responsibility, teach them to be kind to the

opposite sex, respect them, have knowledge about them, teach them to be gentle and honest to self and others, teach forgiveness. (Brian, 36)

The father's responsibility should be unchanged or untouched by divorce. (David, 44)

The responsibility for fathers is, in my opinion, equal to mothers. (Ray, 48)

Children's need for safety and security were paramount for many fathers, and they regarded a strong paternal presence as a main source of protection in their children's lives.

To continue to provide for the needs of the children in the same way as a non-divorced father, without limits, take care of anything and everything, ensure the child is emotionally supported in dealing with issues that threaten the child. (Keith, 37)

To protect them from the outflow from the divorce proceedings. Basically to ensure that they have a safe area to be in psychologically so that they know that they're safe asking questions or expressing their feelings... It really just boils down to giving them as much of a normal life as possible. The difference being that they're trying to cope with the psychological stresses with what's gone on. Trying to alleviate that. (David, 2)

Fathers' view of "responsible fathering" after divorce was one in which, first and foremost, they actively shared with their child's mother the continuing emotional and physical care of their child, and secondarily, they shared in the continuing financial support of their child. Again, it may be noted that fathers saw their responsibilities as addressing children's emotional needs as more important than meeting their physical needs. All eighty-two fathers identified active love and care as a paternal responsibility.

The main responsibilities of a father would be providing emotional, physical and financial love and support. To provide a safe environment when transactions occur between spouses. (Michael, 31)

I would like to take in every aspect of their life and teach and guide and share with them all my life experiences from every... you know, like how they interact with people, how to treat people... you know, how to treat people with respect. (Jim, 22)

Be involved with the children, that means do what you used to do when you were married. You provide for them, you're a caregiver for them, just give them food and shelter. You teach them, you know, you play, bond so that the children know where they come from. They know the importance of the family unit. (Robert, 23)

*Table 4-6 Paternal Responsibilities*

| | Most Important | Top 3 | Total No. Fathers Identifying |
|---|---|---|---|
| Active love, care | 44 | 60 | 82 |
| Being there | | | |
| Access; spending time, engagement | | | |
| Respect for children's needs | 16 | 32 | 40 |
| Other roles: teacher, guide, role model | | | |
| Safety, security, protection | 5 | 22 | 24 |
| Emotional development | 5 | 11 | 13 |
| Food, shelter, clothing | 3 | 18 | 28 |
| Financial provision | | | |
| Respect for co-parent | 2 | 7 | 7 |
| Mutual respect | | | |

Finally, despite the fact that stability and consistency were identified by twenty-five fathers as a core need of children after divorce, fathers did not see the provision of stability and consistency as lying within the paternal realm of responsibility, as much as they did within the realm of social institutional responsibility. Table 4-6 summarizes fathers' views of their parental responsibilities vis-à-vis their children's needs during the divorce transition.

Fathers were also asked about the responsibilities of social institutions in relation to the ongoing father-child relationship. Table 4-7 lists, first, which responsibility of social institutions fathers reported to be the most important in relation to the ongoing father-child relationship, then which responsibilities of social institutions were reported as among the three most important, and then the sum total of all responsibilities of social institutions identified.

The responsibilities of social institutions, according to fathers, are primarily to support fathers in the fulfillment of their parenting responsibilities, by means of equality and fairness in court-determined post-divorce parenting arrangements, with fathers recognized as having equal rights and responsibilities as mothers vis-à-vis their children.

Social institutions need to recognize the father as an equal parent. (Craig, 10)

I think they have a responsibility to promote fathering, promote the maintenance of father-child relationships. (Theo, 18)

*Table 4-7 Social Institutional Responsibilities*

|  | Most Important | Top 3 | Total No. Fathers Identifying |
|---|---|---|---|
| Legal rights | 24 | 42 | 51 |
| Shared parenting, equal access | | | |
| Recognition of father as parent | 14 | 31 | 33 |
| Respect, validation | | | |
| Removing gender bias | 8 | 24 | 30 |
| Dealing with parental alienation | | | |
| Dealing with false allegations, shaping positive image | | | |
| Mediation, counselling | 7 | 12 | 20 |
| Remove adversarial system/court | | | |
| Mediation as an alternative | | | |
| Support services for fathers | 6 | 26 | 33 |
| BIOC = children's needs | 6 | 13 | 17 |
| Access enforcement | 5 | 8 | 12 |

Courts need to see that there's two parents, not just one parent. (Stephen, 24)

Second, fundamental to fathers is the need for all social institutions involved in the lives of children and families to recognize fathers as parents of equal value, status and importance in children's lives as mothers.

Recognize that fathers have valid concerns and inputs, give credit to fathers, acknowledge, respect and support them. (Wren, 27)

I think firstly they have to recognize the fathers as parents. (Keith, 16)

Equitable treatment by the judicial system and the recognition of the role of the father and the importance of the role of the father. (John, 11)

Number one, not to take an attitude that the father is the second-rate parent. Now those are strong words but it's true I think. I did deal with social workers who took that attitude, and I dealt with courts with that attitude. (Bruce, 3)

I think the most important thing is for them to understand that parents, although different, each fulfill crucial roles in the development of children. (Hal, 25)

Third is removing gender bias in the court system, which is reported by fathers as firmly entrenched, with poor outcomes for the ongoing father-child relationship in disputed child custody cases. This includes dealing effectively with the problems of parental alienation and false allegations.

> I'd have to say that whenever any of these persons in authority are examining a situation that from the beginning they have to set aside their biases. (Steve, 61)

> They have the responsibility of educating, of making sure children are protected against abusive parents... but they also need to make sure that they don't overstep their boundaries and that they don't create conflict... or cause conflict or pursue false allegations. (Paul, 12)

> We need to drop the idea that dads are somehow the bad guys. We have all these stereotypes about "dead-beat dads" or dads being abusers, molesters, that they're not gentle or nurturing. (Brad, 5)

Fathers indicated that access to mediation for parents during the separation and divorce transition is fundamental. Fathers also stressed that support services for fathers are largely absent and should be available.

> The same services they provide to the women in the same situation should be available to men to the same extent, in the same degree, period. In other words equal treatment of divorced mothers and divorced fathers in all respects, including financial and emotional. (Chuck, 60)

> To assist children and their parents in a context of caring, compassion and equality to fulfill the needs of the children, first and foremost. (Brian, 20)

Most important for fathers, however, in regard to the responsibilities of social institutions, is reform of the legal sole custody system — in the direction of equal shared parenting. Access enforcement was regarded as an important first step in this regard.

> Responsibilities as legislated would include equal parenting, with the children, which would encompass daily contact. (Rob, 46)

> The main thing for me would be ensuring that kids have access to their father. (Joe, 1)

> Defiance of court-ordered access: I think that should absolutely not be tolerated by the judicial system. (Steve, 68)

In discussing social institutional responsibilities, fathers emphasized that the legal system has largely failed to effectively address post-divorce parenting disputes. As mothers were the petitioners in the legal divorce proceedings in most cases, fathers often felt on the defensive in regard to their own legal rights. They were not prepared for the loss of their children from their care; rather than supporting the father, the court effectively removed him as an engaged parent via a sole maternal custody or primary maternal residence order. Fathers reported an almost complete lack of social institutional support for their parental role.

Fathers were asked what helped and hindered their relationship with their children after divorce, and to identify the most salient issues facing divorced fathers today. In regard to what most hindered the post-divorce father-child relationship, the court system and their former partners were identified; fathers felt vulnerable as a result of mothers' gatekeeping function in regard to the father-child relationship. It was thus not surprising that fathers identified the cooperation of their ex-partners as co-parents as most helpful in preserving their attachment to their children; court system reform and shared parenting legislation were seen to be the next most helpful.

Finally, fathers were asked to identify what they perceived were the main issues facing divorced fathers today. In regard to these core issues, simple lack of access to children was identified by a large majority, fifty-six of the eighty-two fathers (see Table 4-8).

Lack of ability to be a parent, because the court ordered that a father can't be a parent. (Jim, 26)

Denial of access is rampant and is effecting fathers in a great way... I believe that by denying fathers access, the judiciary is not applying the law equally. It allows for one parent to dictate over the other parent

*Table 4-8 Main Issues Facing Divorced Fathers*

|  | Top 3 | Total No. Fathers Identifying |
|---|---|---|
| Lack of access to children | 44 | 56 |
| Inequality in legal system, gender bias | 38 | 46 |
| Court/legal reform: lack of recognition of father, adversarial system | 30 | 33 |
| Financial consequences, child support inequity | 21 | 22 |
| Parental alienation | 4 | 30 |

> the terms of the relationship between the children and the parent. (Manfred, 49)

> Losing the relationship, that was my most important issue, losing the relationship with my children. (James, 52)

This was followed closely by the issue of inequality and gender bias in the legal system, cited by forty-six fathers. From the standpoint of fathers, lack of access to children is the result of gender bias and legal inequities in the judicial system.

> Being treated as equal, having access to the kids. It's a hard one, because being recognized as a parent would probably automatically take care of that, and that sadly is not the case. That just doesn't seem to be accepted. (David, 2)

> The bias that fathers have to deal with, the biases in the court system, the adversarial system, the lack of political will, the lack of empathy, the lack of funding to support the needs of families, the divorce industry, the lack of awareness. (Avi, 69)

Related to the issue of gender bias in the family law system, thirty-three fathers identified an urgent need for legal system reform.

> I feel the family court system is absolutely, without question, the wrong arena, the wrong forum, for family disputes... The system is a huge, huge, huge, problem. Again, from social services, right up to the judges themselves, with everything in between. (Preston, 7)

> The court system, because it doesn't work. Like, they can make a decision that this should be the way it is, but people like my ex-wife, they just don't do it and that's it. Nothing happens; they do as they please, end of story. (Brian, 9)

> We need to establish a truly gender-inclusive legislative regime based on presumptive equal shared parenting. (Brian, 20)

> I guess just how the divorce procedure is, that it's based on fighting one another. And because of the focus on the money, the kids can end up being "pawns," you know, they can end up in the middle and then you're not thinking about their needs. (Tom, 6)

Thirty fathers identified parental alienation and paternal estrangement from children as a core issue, related to their ex-partners' lack of support and undermining of the father-child relationship, maternal alignment with children against the father, mother-child enmeshment and legal system constraints.

> The custodial parent, if they are negatively influencing the children, that is probably the biggest thing. (Craig, 10)

> I believe that by the judiciary not treating the law equally it allows for one parent to dictate over the other parent the terms of the relationship between children and parents. (Manfred, 49)

Access denial is a feature of such alienation, as is the court system's lack of enforcement of paternal access. Access denial and parental alienation were described as forms of parental and child abuse by fathers.

> It was actually quite astounding to me that I didn't have any rights in the situation, that she could just unilaterally decide that I couldn't see the kids and there wasn't anything I could do. (Theo, 18)

> I don't care how many orders I've got in my hand they're worth shit for lack of a better word, they're not worthy of anything, they're simply instruments of torture to children which is not one of the roles, of my role as a good father. (Alan, 33)

Fathers felt powerless to address the issues of access denial and parental alienation. Many had unsuccessfully sought legal redress; others had simply given up in this regard, having come to believe that their efforts would be in vain. The legal imbalance of power in favour of custodial mothers and the potential for disruption of father-child attachments were a concern for many fathers, who described "legal abuse" in terms of courts and other social institutions reinforcing the power imbalance between custodial mothers and non-custodial fathers.

> The whole legal system being heavily weighted in favour of women. As a result, the focus is not on the kids. (Chuck, 60)

> The power imbalance between custodial and non-custodial parents — that's what I think is the number one core issue. Because it allows for the abuse of one parent by the other. (Randy, 76)

> Unfortunately, the laws are manipulated to favour one parent over the other. And in order to make the adversarial system work you have to destroy the bond between one parent and the child. (Steve, 61)

> So, instead of going to all out trial with a lawyer, you know, and appealing and all that kind of stuff, I just relented. (Brian, 20)

As we have seen, fathers' frustrations with the legal system were prevalent in their divorce narratives. "Jumping through legal hoops" seemed an endless task; resistance to and cooperation with the legal system both resulted in poor outcomes for the post-divorce father-child relationship, as fathers' legal rights were rarely recognized.

The remedies suggested by fathers include a legal presumption of shared parenting or joint physical custody, legal access enforcement and mandatory family mediation. Sixty-nine of the eighty-two fathers were in favour of some form of mandatory mediation.

Before we turn to a discussion of these remedies in the next chapter, I include here a brief word about mothers who find themselves in a similar situation to the fathers I interviewed: involuntarily relinquishing non-custodial mothers. Although the subject of this book is divorced fathers, the experiences and effects of child absence are virtually identical for the increasing number of mothers who find themselves in the situation of being removed as custodial parents of their children after divorce. During the course of my research on divorced fathers, I was approached by a mutual aid group of non-custodial mothers in southwestern British Columbia who wanted the opportunity to participate as respondents in the research project. I subsequently replicated the divorced fathers study with a group of fourteen of these mothers (Kruk 2010b), asking them about their divorce experiences, and their perspectives of their children's needs, their responsibilities as mothers and the responsibilities of social institutions to support non-custodial mothers as parents. I wanted to test out whether the views of non-custodial mothers and fathers are similar or different in regard to child custody.

As far as children's needs are concerned, according to both mothers and fathers, children need a stable and unthreatened parental (not "access" or visiting) relationship with both their parents; and they need to be loved, and in no way to feel to blame for their parents' divorce. More fathers than mothers identified security and protection as a basic need; whereas inter-parental cooperation and respect were identified more frequently by mothers, as were children's needs for stability and consistency in their routines and relationships.

As far as parental responsibilities are concerned, virtually all of both fathers and mothers cited the responsibility to *be there for their kids*, in some form of loving parental capacity. For mothers, this was followed closely by respect toward the other parent; for fathers, this was followed closely by the notion that fathers basically have only one responsibility: respect for their children's needs. A large number of fathers identified fathers' responsibility for ensuring the safety, security and protection of their children; this was not cited by mothers as a core maternal responsibility.

As to the responsibilities of social institutions, there were some minor differences in perspectives of fathers and mothers; however, both mothers and fathers agreed about the primary importance of supporting *both* parents to be responsible parents. According to the mothers, this must be done through supporting parents to be responsive to their children's needs, in the manner that parents identify those needs.

Finally, an important finding from my research is that when mothers and fathers are both situated as non-custodial parents, there are virtually no differences between the genders with respect to child custody; both seek a shared parental responsibility presumption in law, which would guarantee both parents meaningful access and routine involvement in their children's lives. A striking finding was the degree to which mothers in particular indicated a preference for an equal or shared parenting arrangement after divorce, as opposed to sole maternal custody or other arrangement. They were asked: "When parents are in dispute about parenting arrangements, what position do you think the law should take which would best meet children's core needs?" Twelve of the fourteen mothers (86 percent) indicated equal or shared parenting (defined as children spending either equal or at least 40 percent of their residential time with each parent after divorce), compared to sixty-four of eighty-two fathers (78 percent).

In sum, our data demonstrate the degree to which divorced fathers experience significant emotional hardship at the time of divorce and after. For these fathers, divorce presents a role strain not comparable to that of most mothers: the possible loss of one's children. The fathers in this study saw their paternal responsibilities as connected to their children's needs for parental involvement and attachment, safety and protection, emotional needs and physical needs, in that order. Fathers' view of "responsible fathering" after divorce was one in which they actively shared with their child's mother the continuing emotional and physical care of their child, as well as financial support. There seems little doubt that current laws and social institutional policies and practices present barriers to responsible fatherhood involvement and father-child attachment after divorce. The adversarial system exacerbates conflict via the "winner takes all" approach, reflected in sole custody or primary residence orders being made when parents cannot agree on post-divorce parenting arrangements.

Chapter 5

# A New Framework for
# Child Custody Determination

Where do we go with respect to law reform in regard to child custody after divorce? The findings from this study of divorced fathers complement the new research findings on children and families experiencing divorce reported in Chapter 2 and point to the urgent need for reform in two main areas: (1) child custody outcomes, toward equal rights and responsibilities between mothers and fathers, as children need to preserve their relationships with both parents if they are to adapt well to the consequences of divorce; and (2) the child custody process, moving away from adversarial resolution toward the use of non-adversarial processes such as mediation.

Fathers were patently clear and united about one point: the legal system is the problem. In particular, adversarial divorce and sole custody decisions are problematic for both children and parents, as the "winner takes all" sole custody framework removes a loving parent from children's lives and exacerbates conflict between separating parents. Within the present legal framework, not only are fathers' responsibilities to their children overlooked by the legal system (apart from their financial obligations), but the responsibilities of social institutions to support fathers are left unaddressed. In this context, it is important to note that courts do not in fact award custody to one or the other parent after divorce; courts remove custody from one parent, as both parents share custody while living together. This is evident in provincial legislation, such as the Family Relations Act in British Columbia. Section 27 (1) of the Act states: "Whether or not married to each other and for so long as they live together, the mother and father of a child are joint guardians unless a tribunal of competent jurisdiction otherwise orders," meaning that when parents live together they share parental duties. Upon separation, according to section 27 (2), "the one of them who usually has care and control of the child is sole guardian of the person of the child." In cases where the parents have never lived together or shared joint guardianship, the mother is the sole guardian of the child. The same statutory regime also applies to custody. The Family Relations Act thus removes joint parenting rights and responsibilities upon parental separation and essentially imposes sole custody. The legal assumption is that only one parent "usually has care and control of the child" and that sole custody is in fact in "the best interests of the child."

There is a realistic and viable alternative to sole custody, both reported in the literature and implemented in a number of jurisdictions worldwide: a rebuttable legal presumption of joint physical custody, also known as equal parenting. An equal parenting presumption (defined as children spending 50 percent of their time with each parent in the absence of family violence or a finding that a child is in need of protection from a parent) is, on the basis of the research evidence, associated with the most salutary outcome for children of divorce and needs to be recognized in legislation.

It needs to be asked why there have been so many barriers placed in the way of shared parenting by legal policymakers, despite the fact that there is both strong public support for shared parenting and research evidence that supports this option as in children's best interests. The simple answer may be that child custody law reform is not in the interests of those who profit from adversarial divorce — and the profits are great, as fully 40 percent of Canadian courts' time is taken up with child custody and access matters.

The responsibilities of social institutions to support parents in the fulfillment of their parenting responsibilities is the overlooked issue in the child custody debate, and yet this may be the key question to consider in any examination of alternative approaches to resolving custody and access impasses between divorcing parents. "Parent blaming," which focuses on parental deficits rather than on their capacities and potentialities, deflects attention and accountability away from the responsibilities of legal and social welfare institutions. Holding parents responsible for what are essentially systemic inequities is an indicator and symptom of such lack of accountability of those institutions charged with supporting parents in their role as parents.

One of the principal findings of my research is that fathers who wish to maintain a responsible, active parental role in the care of their children are prevented from doing so. The removal of custody and the establishment of a new "access" relationship is a major barrier to responsible fatherhood after divorce and fathers' ongoing relationships with their children. Thus, another question to consider is: Why are parents with no civil or criminal wrongdoing to their children forced to surrender their responsibility to raise their children? What justifies the court system's removal of parental rights and responsibilities to raise their children?

From a children's rights and children's interests perspective, the following questions remain unasked:

- On what basis do courts justify treating parents unequally (one as the custodial and the other as the non-custodial parent), under the guise of the "best interests of the child"? How is it in the best interests of the child to see one parent denigrated as a secondary "accessory" parent? From a child-centred perspective, does this dishonour one of their parents?

- On what basis do courts justify discriminating against children of divorce by using the indeterminate "best interests of the child" standard, which allows judges with little or no training in child development and family dynamics, unfettered discretion to remove a parent from their lives, as opposed to the more rigorous "child in need of protection" standard for children from non-divorced families? The "best interests of the child" standard has long been recognized by legal scholars as an indeterminate standard, in contrast to the "child in need of protection" standard, where there are clear guidelines for social workers to investigate abuse complaints, and only a thorough investigation and a finding that a child is in need of protection warrants parental removal.

- Is the removal of a parent from the life of a child, via legal sole custody, itself a form of parental alienation? Is a legal sole custody determination in the absence of a child protection finding a form of legal abuse of children — and thus a child welfare matter? Is this a form of child abuse, given that one of children's primary attachments are broken and their core needs violated, that sole custody exposes children to increased conflict and that a viable alternative exists in the form of equal shared parenting?

The U.N. Convention on the Rights of the Child, to which Canada is a signatory, may be instructive in this regard. Two key principles underlying the Convention are that parents have the primary responsibility for nurturing children, and the role of governments and communities is to support children and their families; these are both seen to be in the "best interests" of children. Article 2 of the Convention stipulates that a child should be protected from all forms of discrimination, including the marital status of his or her parents. This means that different legal standards regarding removal of parents should not be applied to children of divorced and those of non-divorced families. Article 5 emphasizes the primacy of parents in their children's lives ("States Parties shall respect the responsibilities, rights and duties of parents..."), Article 8 stipulates the child's right to preserve his or her family and cultural identity, and Article 9 states that children shall not be separated from their parents against their will. Article 18 indicates that both parents have the primary responsibility for the upbringing and development of the child, and that states shall render appropriate assistance to parents in the performance of their child-rearing responsibilities. Article 19 of the Convention refers to needed measures to protect children from all forms of violence, injury or abuse, neglect, maltreatment or exploitation — and it refers to actual violence and maltreatment, not risks of violence and maltreatment. To remove child custody from a parent because of "risk" rather than proof of harm is not in keeping with the Convention. And removing a loving parent exposes children to greater risk of harm. In removing custody from a parent in the absence of child abuse and an investigated finding that a child is in need of protection, Canadian courts and governments appear to be in violation of the U.N. Convention.

Replacing sole custody with equal parenting in legislation, a solution that will simplify that which is unnecessary complex in child custody disputes, would state simply: when parents cannot agree on parenting arrangements after separation or divorce, their children will spend equal time in their mother's and their father's households. Rather than being forced to prove the unfitness of the other parent in their quest to "win" custody, parents would be expected to work through the development of a shared parenting plan and schedule, which provides an incentive to negotiate and cooperate, rather than compete for their children. Underlying shared parenting as an alternative framework of child custody determination are the following three core principles:

1. children need both parents routinely involved in their care, not as "visitors" in their lives;
2. parents are primarily responsible to meet their children's needs, as they are the real experts on their children's best interests; and
3. social institutions such as the courts are responsible to support parents in the fulfillment of their parenting responsibilities.

Current law, policy and judicial practice effectively relieve parents of their parental responsibilities.

## A Four Pillar Framework of Child Custody Determination

The question remains: How do we make a presumption of shared parental responsibility a reality? Legislating shared parenting as the norm is only a beginning. A "four pillar" framework to child custody determination, which incorporates harm reduction, treatment, prevention and enforcement, is needed (see Table 5-1).

### Pillar 1: Harm Reduction

First is the harm reduction pillar. What unites most divorcing parents is the importance of shielding their children from harm, as reducing harm is most in keeping with the needs of children. The first pillar would establish a legal expectation that existing parent-child relationships will continue after separation. This is in the interests of children preserving their primary attachments to both their parents, maintaining stability in children's relationships with their parents, maximizing parental cooperation and reducing conflict, and preventing serious family violence and exposing

---

*Table 5-1 Shared Parenting after Divorce*

A 4-Pillar Framework

Harm reduction
    Rebuttable legal presumption of shared parental responsibility in disputed child custody cases
    Treatment
        Parenting plans
        Therapeutic family mediation
        More intensive support in high conflict cases
    Prevention
        Shared parenting education
    Enforcement
        Judicially determined custody arrangements in cases where family violence is a factor
        Judicially determined custody arrangements in cases of non-compliance with shared parenting

---

children to violence. Post-divorce parenting arrangements would be expected to reflect pre-divorce parenting arrangements in regard to the relative amount of time each parent spends with the children. In cases of dispute, however, shared parenting, defined as children spending equal time with each of their parents, would be the legal presumption, in the absence of established family violence or child abuse. This would provide judges with a clear guideline and would avoid the dilemma of judges adjudicating children's "best interests" in the absence of expertise in this area. It would divert parents from a destructive court battle over their children's care and would provide an incentive for parents to engage in therapeutic family mediation focused on the development of cooperative parenting plans. It would convey the view that mothers and fathers are of equal status before the law in regard to their parental rights and responsibilities and convey to children the message that their parents are of equal value and have equal legal status as parents.

   Although children spending equal time with each of their parents may not always reflect the existing arrangements in the pre-separation household, shared parental responsibility is in keeping with current caregiving patterns, as the majority of mothers and fathers are now sharing responsibility for child care in two-parent families. A legal presumption of shared parental responsibility is thus a more individualized approach than the "one size fits all" formula of sole custody, a blunt instrument that removes a parent from the life of a child in contested cases. If parents cannot agree on caregiving arrangements after divorce, an individualized approach in which post-separation parenting approximating as closely as possible the existing arrangements in the two-parent family is recommended, in the interest of stability for children. It is only in those cases where both parents present as primary caregivers that the shared parenting presumption would apply, in the interests of decreasing conflict and ensuring that each parent remains involved.

### Pillar 2: Treatment

Shared parental responsibility is radically different from the dominant approach of sole custody, and its likelihood of success as a new approach is significantly increased with meaningful supports in place. At the same time, the likelihood of success of support services like therapeutic family mediation is increased with shared parenting as the cornerstone of family law, as it provides parents with an incentive to negotiate on an equal footing.

Thus, the second pillar would be that of treatment, which includes facilitating the development of parenting plans, mediation and more intensive support in high conflict cases. Unlike the present legal approach of discouraging open communication between parents on child care matters, which leads to polarization, such support would be focused on assisting parents to jointly develop a parenting plan before any court hearing is held. The court's role would then be to legally ratify the negotiated plan. Through direct negotiation, parent education programs, mediation or lawyer negotiation, a detailed parenting plan that delineates parenting schedules and all of the parental responsibilities that meet the needs of children would be established within a legal framework of shared parental responsibility. A legal shared parenting presumption would provide an incentive for parents to use mediation rather than adversarial means to settle child custody matters, because mediation would be seen as facilitating the development of an equal parenting plan.

Parent education regarding children's needs and interests during and after the divorce transition, followed by a therapeutic approach to divorce mediation, offers a highly effective and efficient means of facilitating the development of cooperative shared parenting plans. Within such an approach, parent education may be used to introduce the option of shared parenting as a viable alternative and to reduce parents' anxiety about this new living arrangement. Mediation would then help parents work through the development and implementation of the parenting plan in as cooperative a manner as possible.

Mediation, as an alternative method of dispute resolution, has considerable and as yet untapped potential in establishing shared parenting as the norm, rather than the exception, for divorced families. In the majority of so-called "high conflict" cases, both parents are capable and loving caregivers and have at least the potential to minimize their conflict and cooperate with respect to their parenting responsibilities within a shared parenting framework. Social institutional support for parents in the implementation of a shared parenting plan is especially critical for these high-conflict couples, where children may be caught in the middle of disputes between parents. There are a number of existing models of therapeutic post-divorce support for such high-conflict families (Dodds 2005), including Garber's (2004) Direct Co-parenting Intervention Model and Lebow's (2003) Integrative Family Therapy Model.

*Pillar 3: Prevention*
Largely missing in divorced family support services today are prevention programs, which would constitute the third pillar. Shared parenting education, within the high school system, in marriage preparation courses and before divorce, is an essential element of a much-needed preventive program of parent education and support. Public education about various models of shared parenting, including models for "high conflict" couples, would replace the current focus on seeking partisan legal representation in an effort to "win" the custody of one's children.

Shared parenting education should also involve the judiciary, as the effects of changes in family law legislation on the actual practices of judges are uncertain. The extent to which legislative reform can bring about the desired result will depend largely on the attitudes of the judiciary as well as those of legal practitioners. Assumptions about shared parenting being unworkable in cases of disputed custody and sole custody being in children's best interests in these cases should be challenged, and stereotypes about disputing parents should be addressed.

*Pillar 4: Enforcement*
Finally, we are left with the problem of how post-separation parenting arrangements are to be monitored and enforced. This would apply both to enforcing shared parenting arrangements and to providing for judicially determined arrangements in cases where family violence is a factor.

The issue of family violence lies at the centre of debates regarding child custody and access, and shared parenting. Although some claim that joint custody endangers women and children, it is clear from current research that shared parenting prevents parental abuse (Bauserman 2002), as 46 percent of first-time violence happens after separation, within the adversarial sole custody system (Ellis and Wight-Peasley 1986; Hotton 2003). As the threat of losing one's children heightens fear and fuels anger, such outcomes are not surprising. A legal shared parental responsibility presumption will prevent violence in cases where there is no prior history of violence, as both parents continue to be equally valued and involved in children's lives and their parental role and identity are in no way threatened. In cases where violence is present and has been established via criminal conviction or a finding that a child is in need of protection, however, shared parenting is not appropriate (Jaffe, Crooks, and Bala 2005).

A legal presumption of shared parenting would either have to be rebuttable in cases of investigated and substantiated child abuse (which includes children witnessing the abuse of a parent) or, as the National Association of Women and the Law (Ontario Women's Network on Custody and Access 2001) has recommended, a rebuttable presumption against shared parental responsibility in cases of family violence and child abuse is needed. Exempt from a shared parenting presumption would be those cases involving either a criminal conviction, such as assault, in a matter directly related to the parenting of the children or a finding by a statutory child welfare authority that a child is in need of protection from a parent. These cases would require judicial determination of child custody, which would consider the importance of preserving children's relationships with their extended family, who could stand in place of the parent deemed unfit to parent.

When spousal abuse or family violence allegations are made, an immediate and thorough investigation of the allegations must be undertaken by a competent child welfare authority. Child exposure to spousal violence should be a legal basis for finding a child in need of protection. Spousal violence is a criminal matter, and allegations of family violence should be part of a criminal and child protection process, not left to be settled in family court. The family court should not have to resolve conflicting criminal allegations, as litigants are entitled to more than "proof on the balance of probabilities" when their relationship with their children is at stake. Family courts should not function as "quasi-criminal" courts; family violence is a criminal matter that must be dealt with in criminal court.

When a shared parenting arrangement is legally ordered, and a parent refuses to abide by the order, disrupting the other parent's time with the children, enforcement measures will be required. Wherever possible, however, mediation should be encouraged in cases where shared parenting orders are breached. It is expected that breaches are less likely when both parents have an active role to play in children's lives within a shared parenting arrangement.

When enforcement measures are necessary, solutions may involve reduction or loss of parenting time, or the following sanctions: a requirement that a parent comply with "make-up" contact if contact has been missed through a breach of an order, compensation for reasonable expenses incurred due to a breach of an order and legal costs against the party that has breached the order. The court should have discretion to impose a bond for all breaches of orders.

Access denial and parental alienation need to be recognized and treated as forms of child abuse. However, what should not be overlooked is that the adversarial sole custody "winner takes all" system is the source of most parental alienation — again, the tendency is to "parent blame" rather than holding the system to account.

In sum, to legally remove a parent from the life of a child, the application of a radically different standard for children of divorced families and for children in two-parent families is clearly discriminatory and therefore unacceptable. The "child in need of protection" standard should be applied to all children, as opposed to the present discriminatory practice of applying the indeterminate "best interests of the child" standard only to children of divorce, which allows judges to remove a fit and loving parent from their lives where no form of violence or abuse is present. The only justification for such parental removal should be a finding that a child is in need of protection from a parent.

# Chapter 6

# Promoting Responsible Fatherhood after Divorce

The subject matter of this book — the lived experiences of divorced fathers and fathers' perceptions of their children's needs and "best interests," and corresponding parental and social institutional responsibilities during and after divorce — is a topic previously unexplored in both fatherhood and divorce research. The focus on children's needs in the study, in contrast to the dominant rhetoric of fathers' and mothers' rights in mainstream analyses, represents a paradigm shift toward a responsibility-to-needs perspective of the contentious and contested concept of the "best interests of the child." Although it is clear from the fathers' accounts reported here that both paternal rights and responsibilities are important to them, children's needs and paternal and social institutional responsibilities to those needs are of uppermost concern to divorced fathers as they struggle to maintain their relationship with their children in the context of a diminished parental identity.

In its aim to promote responsible fatherhood involvement after divorce, this book focuses on the unasked questions in current child custody debates: what are the core needs of children in the divorce transition, the responsibilities of fathers to those needs, and the responsibilities of social institutions to support parents in the fulfillment of their parental obligations? The responsibilities of representatives of social institutions, including the legal and child welfare systems, have been almost completely overlooked within current child custody debates, which have tended to adopt a deficit-based "parent blaming" orientation to divorce practice and policymaking, most evident in the case of divorced fathers.

The following new findings emerged in the present study that challenge myths, stereotypes and the "practice wisdom" prevalent within the divorce arena:

1.  Given family law reform rhetoric that Canadian courts are making joint custody decrees in contested child custody cases, one of our more significant findings was that a marked discontinuity exists between pre- and post-divorce parent-child living arrangements, more marked than in earlier studies, in the direction of equal or shared parenting before divorce shifting to sole maternal custody after. Whereas thirty-eight of eighty-two fathers reported shared parenting arrangements before divorce, only

eleven fathers reported shared parenting arrangements after divorce. Twenty fathers reported primary maternal care arrangements before divorce, and sixty-five reported primary maternal care arrangements afterwards. This challenges the view that courts have moved beyond sole custody determinations; in fact, despite legal designations of "joint custody," in an increasing number of cases, fathers are routinely being removed as primary caregivers of their children by the courts when parents cannot agree on post-divorce parenting arrangements. Although outcomes vary from one legal jurisdiction to another, the outcomes for fathers in regard to maintaining father-child relationships in contested child custody cases clearly appear to be worsening.

2.   I also found that the effects of child absence on fathers who lose their children and their parental role via sole custody or maternal residence decrees are now more pronounced, as fathers' involvement with, attachment to and influence on their children before divorce have increased. Twenty years ago I discovered, contrary to the prevailing image of the "deadbeat dad," that fathers who lost contact with their children suffered a grief reaction containing all the elements of a bereavement. Today they are manifesting a more pronounced reaction of full-blown post-traumatic stress. Their storied accounts contain predominant themes of grief and loss, broken attachments, access denial, parental alienation, non-existent support services, the adversarial system heightening conflict, legal abuse, false allegations, financial losses and, for a minority of fathers, positive outcomes. The large number of fathers volunteering to tell their stories in this study challenges the view that involuntarily disengaged fathers are now fewer in number and that courts are taking into account the history of parental child care involvement in child custody decision-making.

3.   The study revealed one key finding previously unreported in the father involvement literature: divorced fathers define the "best interests" of their children in terms of their children's needs, and in most cases children's emotional, psychological, social, moral and spiritual needs are seen to prevail over their physical (financial) needs. Fathers are acutely aware that their children's emotional well being in particular is compromised by father absence. Their perspective is in line with both father absence research and the recent UNICEF report on the well being of children in economically advanced nations, in which Canada's children were found to be faring poorly, less as a result of material poverty as poverty of parental involvement, attachment and influence in their lives. In regard to emotional well being, Canada's children rank eighteenth out of the twenty-one countries studied in regard to child depression and suicide, substance abuse, violence and risk-taking, early engagement in

sexual activity, addiction and youth crime. All of these are closely linked to father absence in a range of research studies. This finding stands in contrast to the dominant view that fathers are more concerned with their legal rights and entitlements than with their children's well being.

4. Fathers consider themselves as having a primary responsibility to address their children's social, emotional, psychological, moral and spiritual needs, as opposed to their material and financial needs, and believe that parental responsibilities to both children's physical/financial and metaphysical/ emotional needs should be equally shared by both parents. This finding challenges the dominant view that fathers' primary responsibility to their children is one of financial provision and child support, and supporting the mother as the primary guardian of children's emotional needs. It also goes counter to laws, policies and practices that foreground fathers' financial responsibilities as central to "child support" after divorce. Fathers consider their children's needs and paternal responsibilities as core elements of father-child attachment, with children's needs for paternal involvement and their emotional needs for love, safety and security as falling within the paternal arena of responsibility.

5. According to fathers, social institutions have a primary responsibility to support fathers, and all parents, in the fulfillment of their parental responsibilities to their children's needs. Yet the main message emerging from the fathers in this study is that the legal system is the problem, as it undermines rather than supports them as active and responsible parents in their children's lives. According to fathers, legislation and social institutional policies and practices get in the way of responsible fatherhood after divorce. In particular, adversarial divorce and "win-lose" court decisions are seen as destructive of not only of co-parental but also parent-child relationships. The adversarial "winner takes all" sole custody framework is seen to exacerbate conflict between parents, and this harms children. According to fathers, the court system is not the forum to deal with co-parenting disputes, despite recent reforms and new programs such as collaborative divorce. Courts routinely remove fathers as primary caregivers, and social welfare institutions are absent as supports for fathers in their struggle to maintain their relationships with their children. Meaningful support services are virtually non-existent for divorced fathers, and a deficit perspective dominates in which fathers are routinely blamed, shamed and cast aside from their legitimate role in their children's lives. According to fathers, social institutions and support services are woefully lacking in support for parents in their parental roles. The lack of valuing and validation of the paternal (and parental) role by social institutions is highly discouraging for fathers in their quest to be responsible parents. Their own sense of parental identity is weakened as

a result, and lack of access to their children and lack of social support for fathering after separation are the conditions within which parental alienation develops, which is largely resistant to therapeutic intervention.

6. Finally, perhaps the most important finding in this study is that socio-legal reform is urgently needed and that inasmuch as it addresses the core needs of children, the most salutary arrangement in cases where parents cannot agree on post-divorce parenting arrangements is that of equal shared parenting, and a legal presumption of shared parental responsibility in these situations is in the best interests of children. Equal or shared parenting is essential to the preservation of father-child attachment bonds and quality of relationships and to responsible fatherhood. Despite this strongly held view, dominant legal policymaking discourse avoids consideration of a shared parental responsibility presumption, and fathers' views of their children's needs and interests are discounted.

The research findings presented here complement recent studies (summarized in Chapter 2) that point to the need for legal and social policy reform in child custody outcomes and the child custody process. The "four-pillar" framework for an equal parenting approach to child custody determination, comprised of harm reduction, treatment, prevention and enforcement, discussed in the previous chapter, presents a logistical framework for socio-legal reform in both spheres.

## Direct Practice with Divorced Fathers

A key point in regard to bringing about needed legal and social policy reforms is that fathers are seeking advocacy support to take direct action in regard to policy change in the child custody arena. Fathers want to be directly involved in law reform efforts and to hold the legal system accountable. As parents, fathers are seeking to reclaim both their authority over and responsibility to their children, in the face of powerful vested interests with a stake in maintaining the status quo.

The influence of vested interest groups (so-called "divorce industry" representatives) was evident during the 2009 Canadian Bar Association meeting in Dublin, Ireland, where Justice Minister Robert Nicholson was confronted by the legal community regarding a private member's bill on shared parenting in the House of Commons. Despite the Conservative Party's stated support for shared parenting as a legal presumption, Nicholson was forced to concede that the "best interests of the child" would remain as the primary consideration in child custody determination, which would maintain judges' power to determine children's best interests in contested custody cases.

In sum, the court system is the major barrier to active and responsible father involvement after separation and divorce. It is supported by a vast bureaucracy that upholds the legal status quo and by the multitude of professionals that work in the shadow of the law. Thus, a consistent pattern of denigration of the claims of fathers is evident from comments such as the following, none of which have any empirical foundation:

> Children's best interests are served by sole custody in contested cases. (Dept. of Justice Canada 1990)

> Joint custody is an attempt of males to continue dominance over females... An essential principle in the high conflict divorce arena is that joint custody and shared parenting plans are not viable resolutions. (Jaffe et al. 2003, 2005)

> Many batterers pursue visitation as a way of getting access to their ex-partners. They may seek custody to engage in prolonged litigation, during which their legal counsel and the court process mirrors the dynamics of the abusive relationship. (Jaffe et al. 2003)

> Divorced fathers have no rights, only responsibilities. (former Canadian Minister of Justice Martin Cauchon, quoted by CanWest News Service 2003)

A large hurdle for divorced fathers is garnering public and political attention and support to deal with the social problems of fatherlessness, parental alienation and diminished father involvement after parental separation and divorce. These problems need to be made more visible, and constructive solutions promoted. Engaging the legal system and professional service providers in dealing with these issues is a huge challenge. A constructive role for these professionals needs to be advanced if family law is to remove itself from the adversarial arena and embrace an equal parenting presumption.

Engaging divorced fathers in professional services remains a challenge, as researchers have described a lack of "fit" between fathers and professional service providers, emanating from two sources: the characteristics of men and fathers themselves (their resistance to counselling and therapy) and aspects of the therapeutic process (which have failed to successfully engage fathers).

Patterns of traditional gender-role socialization directing men toward self-sufficiency and control, independent problem-solving and emotional restraint have largely worked against fathers being able to acknowledge personal difficulties and request help. Professional service providers do not always consider such psychological obstacles to therapy and thus do not address fathers' unique needs. The research on separated and divorced fathers is clear about their most pressing need: their continued meaningful involvement with their children, as active parents. The lack of recognition of this primary need and a deficit- rather than strengths-based orientation to fathers are the mains reason for therapists' lack of success in engaging divorced fathers. This is the place we must start in reaching out to divorced fathers.

If fathers are to be constructively engaged, their perspective on their own needs and those of their children during the divorce transition must be recognized and acknowledged by policymakers and service providers. A systematic and integrated approach is required to include fathers in research, policy development, and implementation and evaluation of services (Eardley and Griffiths 2009; Father Inclusive Practice Forum 2005).

The following guidelines may assist professionals seeking to engage divorced fathers.

First, an active program of outreach is essential, as fathers report an almost complete lack of support services, and they remain a highly vulnerable population. Fathers who were highly involved with and attached to their children and suddenly find themselves forcefully removed from their children's lives experience trauma writ large. The experience of being removed as a loving parent from the life of one's child via a sole custody order strikes at the heart of one's being. Reported suicide rates are of "epidemic" proportions among divorced fathers struggling to maintain a parenting relationship with their children, and "legal abuse" has been noted in divorced father suicide cases (Kposowa 2000). Ensuring that fathers are not disenfranchised from the lives of their children is suicide prevention, and service providers need to be vigilant regarding symptoms of post-traumatic stress and suicidal ideation among divorced fathers. Again, fathers who do talk about their woundedness are subjected to a mean-spirited cultural response, where all such talk is mocked.

Second, fathers can be supported by means of supporting mothers as co-parents. The norm of sole maternal custody is gradually giving way to shared parenting. But for many mothers, societal expectations that mothers assume primary care and control of children act as a major barrier to shared parenting, despite the obvious benefits for mothers.

Third, fathers will respond positively to services that offer a strengths-based approach that they perceive will benefit their children. Focusing on children's needs and paternal responsibilities in relation to those needs are vitally important to engaging divorced fathers.

Fourth, divorced fathers that are estranged are looking for constructive alternatives to adversarial methods of reconnecting with their children, including therapeutic family mediation. Service providers with a positive orientation to mediation are valued by fathers. Above all else, the key to engaging divorced fathers is to validate their parenting identity and their parenting role; at present, fathers report feeling invalidated as parents by professional service providers. Support for the legal presumption of shared parenting is critically important to fathers; if this is not a practitioner's orientation, this will be a major barrier to service provision. It is also important to recognize the court system and sole custody decisions as major barriers to meaningful fatherhood involvement after divorce.

Fathers who are alienated from their children are a particularly vulnerable population. Feelings of learned helplessness are endemic, evident in sentiments such as "my children are lost to me forever," as despite their best efforts to maintain a parenting role in the lives of their children, fathers are shut out.

Ellis (2005) provides some useful guidelines for practitioners when alienated fathers request help. In these cases, fathers may still have some contact with their children, though it may be brief, infrequent and erratic. At those visits the children may be particularly hostile or rejecting, rebuffing any attempt the father makes to develop a rapport with them. Or he may have had no contact with his children for months or years. He may have had some minimal visitation restored by the courts after a long absence from the children's lives. Regardless of the circumstance, the alienated father must make every effort to erode the image of himself as the "evil villain." He needs to be kind, patient and sympathetic, especially in the face of the child's verbal attacks, acting out and noncompliance, and he must never take such attacks personally. Second, the father must withdraw from any actions that put the children in the middle and cause them to feel they must take sides. This includes making positive statements about and not venting anger toward the mother, even when he feels justified to do so. Third, wherever possible, the alienated father should consider ways in which to mollify the hurt and anguish of the mother and remain open to apology and forgiveness. Fourth, the father must realistically appraise the coalition against him (former friends and extended family) and its strength and look for ways to dismantle the coalition, even convert enemies to allies by extending an olive branch. Finally, the alienated father should be advised to never give up contact altogether, as absence is interpreted by children as abandonment. Contact should never be forced, but small acts of kindness and concern may be offered.

Above all, service providers need to be active in the politics of reform with respect to child custody. The best way to support fathers, according to divorced fathers, is through advocacy and activism. The international equal parenting coalition is a positive social movement, and it is important to educate politicians and lawmakers in this regard.

## Equal Parenting as an International Grassroots Social Movement

The equal parenting movement, comprised of groups such as Fathers for Justice (F4J) in the United Kingdom, the Children's Rights Council in the United States, the Lone Fathers Association in Australia and the Canadian Equal Parenting Coalition, is an international social movement that seeks to avert the many tragedies related to the legal disenfranchisement of fathers from the lives of their children subsequent to divorce. In a stated attempt to arouse the conscience of the community over the specific injustice of the forced removal of capable and loving parents from children's lives via legal sole custody judgments, the movement has grown from a small brigade of activists in the United Kingdom to a broad network of organized protest groups around the world. In Canada and abroad, equal parenting groups have garnered public sympathy and support, and despite official and media condemnation of the nonviolent civil disobedience efforts of this group, resulting in legal charges of mischief, there seems to be public support of their methods as well. A recent Vancouver Province editorial condemned the Vancouver F4J group for causing Vancouver traffic chaos by closing down arterial roads and bridges, and polled readers on their views on the matter. Sixty-six percent of the polled readership supported fathers' methods as a tool to arouse the conscience of the community over the injustice of removing fathers from their children's lives. Similarly a recent British poll asked, "Should Fathers for Justice stop protesting?"; 73 percent indicated that they should carry on.

The calls of equal parenting groups for a legal shared parenting presumption have also contributed to a rise in public support for equal shared parenting across the globe. For example, on the Massachusetts state ballot in the 2004 U.S. federal election, over 80 percent of voters favoured a non-binding shared parenting statute. Specifically, the question was whether they would ask their state representative "to vote for legislation to create a strong presumption in child custody cases in favor of joint physical and legal custody, so that the court will order that children have equal access to both parents as much as possible, except where there is clear and convincing evidence that one parent is unfit, or that joint custody is not possible due to the fault of one of the parents." Since then, referenda in other states have produced similar results. In Canada, a recent government poll obtained almost 80 percent public support for an equal parenting presumption, including cases of high conflict between divorcing parties. The mounting anger and decreased confidence of the public toward a system that continues to apply a "one size fits all" sole custody approach is now routinely reported in public opinion polls (see Braver 2008, Fabricius 2010).

Thus, a number of jurisdictions, including several U.S. states, Australia, the Netherlands and Belgium, have radically revised their family law statutes and legislated some form of shared or equal parenting presumption. Equal parenting groups in these jurisdictions have been instrumental in this effort.

## Responsible Fatherhood: Final Thoughts

We conclude with a return to our main theoretical construct, that of "responsible fatherhood." The fathers in this study saw their paternal responsibilities as connected to children's needs for parental involvement and attachment, safety and protection, emotional needs and physical needs, in that order. Fathers' view of "responsible fatherhood" after divorce was one in which they actively shared with their child's mother the continuing emotional and physical care of their child, as well as financial support.

The prodigious challenges and barriers facing divorced fathers seeking to maintain active and responsible fatherhood represent perhaps the most glaring example of the lack of social institutional support available to parents throughout North America. North American parents in general report not feeling supported in their role by various social institutions, and in such a context they feel isolated and anxious about their parenting responsibilities (Birnbaum, Russell and Clyne 2007). These feelings are more pronounced for divorced parents, who have limited options for dispute resolution when they find themselves at odds over the post-divorce parenting of their children. They are most pronounced for divorced fathers in these circumstances, who are culturally, legislatively and legally disadvantaged with respect to post-divorce parenting and report that they are completely isolated from available support programs.

Post-divorce fathering is influenced by contextual and structural factors to a much greater extent than fathering in the context of the two-parent family. Despite a trend toward egalitarian division of child care responsibility in two-parent families and alternatives to adversarial resolution of divorce-related disputes, divorced fathers involved with the legal system experience significant emotional hardship at the time of divorce and after. For these fathers, divorce presents a significant threat: the possible loss of their children and their parental identity. A father's attachment to and involvement with his children earns approval while he is married, and while these feelings of attachment do not cease upon divorce, his ongoing involvement with his children is placed at risk, as maternal custody remains the dominant post-divorce arrangement for families, with mothers being custodial parents in about 80 percent of contested child custody cases across North America (Gunnoe and Braver 2002a; Kruk, 2005). A principal finding of this study is that fathers who wish to maintain a responsible, active parental role in the care of their children are prevented from doing so by the court system.

Social institutional support is a critical mediating factor in the maintenance of meaningful father-child relationships after divorce and a necessary element in enabling active and responsible fatherhood post-divorce. Yet the responsibilities of social institutions to support fathers in the fulfillment of their parenting responsibilities is not a public issue to any degree and is largely overlooked in current child custody debates, which have focused on the competing rights-based claims of parents. However, a child-focused framework of child custody determination, focused on children's needs, parental responsibilities in regard to these needs and social institutional responsibilities to support parents in the fulfillment of their parental responsibilities may offer a fresh approach to the issue.

Promoting responsible fatherhood and respecting father-child attachments, according to divorced fathers, should be a primary goal of child custody law reform, and this is best accomplished by means of replacing legal sole custody with legal shared parenting orders. Fathers have the motivation and skills to be active and responsible parents after divorce, but are lacking in social institutional policies and practices that support the ongoing father-child relationship.

Fathers' sense of self-efficacy is undermined when they are disregarded as primary caregivers of their children. Without social institutional support, fathers' parental identity is also undermined, and paternal disengagement from children's lives is often the result. The continuation of his role as an active and responsible father is strongly related to whether or not a father perceives his parental identity as validated by social institutional systems. Social institutions thus regulate the father-child relationship; current laws and social institutional policies and practices present formidable barriers to responsible fatherhood involvement and father-child attachment after divorce, as fathers report that their post-divorce parental identity is not validated by social institutional systems.

Commitment to the ethic of responsible fatherhood extends beyond the father, to the mother, to professionals who work with children and families and, importantly, to social institutions entrusted with the support of families (Doherty, Kouneski and Erickson 1998). From fathers' standpoint, current laws, social policies and practices have a profoundly negative effect on father-child relationships. An alternative to the "winner takes all" sole custody model that ensures that both parents maintain a parental role in their children's lives and preserve primary attachments is urgently needed.

A shared parental responsibility approach to child custody determination after divorce strongly warrants consideration, as the indeterminate "best interests of the child" standard has failed to provide an alternative to the sole custody model. I propose a four-pillar framework of child custody determination in this regard, with a rebuttable legal presumption of shared parental responsibility as the first pillar of harm reduction. Divorce education, mediation and post-divorce support for high conflict couples focused on facilitating the development and implementation of shared parenting plans constitute the second treatment pillar, and prevention and enforcement the third and fourth pillars of family law reform.

Both Kelly's (2006) overview of current divorce research and Bauserman's (2002) meta-analysis of the thirty-three major North American studies over the past decade comparing outcomes in joint and sole custody homes found that, on all divorce-specific and general adjustment measures, shared parental responsibility or joint physical custody is associated with more salutary outcomes for children and families. Fabricius (2003), Fabricius and Hall (2000), Parkinson, Cashmore and Single (2005) and Laumann-Billings and Emery (2000), focusing on the perspective of children in divorce, found that equal time with each of their parents is precisely what the majority of children desire and consider to be in their best interests, and most protective of father-child attachments. Shared parenting shields children from conflict between parents, as conflict increases in sole custody and decreases in joint custody families after divorce (Bauserman 2002). Finally, as half of first-time family violence occurs after separation within the context of sole custody (Ellis and Wight-Peasley 1986; Hotton 2003), shared parenting protects children from exposure to violence after parental divorce.

A legal presumption of shared parental responsibility is a realistic and viable option to sole custody, now widely reported in the literature and implemented in a number of jurisdictions worldwide (Kelly 2006; Kruk 2005). Such a presumption preserves primary attachments and ensures that both parents maintain an active and responsible parental role in their children's lives. Shared parental responsibility is in keeping with current caregiving patterns, as shared responsibility for child care has emerged as the norm both in two-parent families and after divorce in non-litigated cases (Bianchi 2000; Higgins and Duxbury 2002; Statistics Canada 2005).

The need for child custody law reform in the direction of shared parental responsibility was identified by the fathers in this study as of paramount importance. Their viewpoint is shared by the majority of parents across North America. Shared parental responsibility is receiving unprecedented public support, with a recent Canadian government poll registering 80 percent public support for a legal presumption.

Without meaningful social institutional supports for shared parenting firmly in place, shared parenting will remain an elusive goal. However, it is problematic to assume that if there are plentiful services and resources in a community, then parents will access them and feel supported, because parents have not been asked what they need to feel supported. Meaningful social institutional supports must start where people are at; it is of paramount importance to give parents the support they say they need. For divorced fathers in particular, there is a disconnection between what service providers are willing to provide and what fathers say they need. Above all, fathers want and need to be listened to and recognized, valued and supported in their role as parents. They crave meaningful community and social institutional support, but those who are responsible for providing necessary support services are not addressing what fathers say are their needs, resulting in fathers' continued sense of isolation. Political and ideological agendas that ignore fathers' stated needs are driving the funding, structure and delivery of services, and fathers are left out.

Imaginative and thoughtful efforts are urgently needed to reach out to all parents who require meaningful support services based on what they identify as their needs. This critical concept, of developing laws, policies and support services "from the parents up," represents a profound shift from current practice, within which professional elites decide which issues and approaches will be the priority. This book is a beginning effort toward such a paradigm shift vis-à-vis divorced fathers and their children.

# Bibliography

Amato, P. 2000. "The Consequences of Divorce for Adults and Children." *Journal of Marriage and Family* 62: 1269–87.

Amato, P.R., and J.G. Gilbreth. 1999. "Non-resident Fathers and Children's Well-Being: A Meta-Analysis." *Journal of Marriage and the Family* 61: 557–73.

Amato, P.R., and B. Keith. 1991. "Parental Divorce and the Well-Being of Children: A Meta-Analysis." *Psychological Bulletin* 110: 26–46.

Arendell, T. 1995. *Fathers and Divorce*. Thousand Oaks, CA: Sage.

Bauserman, R. 2002. "Child Adjustment in Joint Custody Versus Sole Custody Arrangements: A Meta-analytic Review." *Journal of Family Psychology* 16(1): 91–102.

Bender, W.N. 1994. "Joint Custody: The Option of Choice." *Journal of Divorce and Remarriage* 21(3/4): 115–31.

Benjamin, M., and H.H. Irving. 1989. "Shared Parenting: A Critical Review of the Research Literature." *Family and Conciliation Courts Review* 27: 21–35.

Bianchi, S. 2000. "Maternal Employment and Time with Children." *Demography* 37: 401–14.

Bianchi, S., J. Robinson, and M. Milkie. 2006. *Changing Rythms of the American Family*. New York: Sage.

Biller, H. 1993. *Fathers and Families*. Westport, CT: Auburn House.

Birnbaum, N., C. Crill Russell, and G. Clyne. 2007. *Vital Communities, Vital Support: How Well Do Canada's Communities Support Parents of Young Children?* Toronto: Invest in Kids.

Bisnaire, L, P. Firestone, and D. Rynard. 1990. "Factors Associated with Academic Achievement in Children Following Parental Separation." *American Journal of Orthopsychiatry* 60(1).

Blankenhorn, D. 1995. *Fatherless America: Confronting Our Most Urgent Social Problem*. New York: Basic Books.

Braver, S. 1998. *Divorced Dads: Shattering the Myths*. New York: Tarcher, Putnam.

Braver, S.L., et al. 2008. "The Court of Public Opinion." Paper presented at the annual conference of the Association of Family and Conciliation Courts, Vancouver.

Brayfield, A. 2003. "Juggling Jobs and Kids." *Journal of Marriage and Family* 57: 321–32.

Brotsky, M., S. Steinman, and S. Zemmelman. 1988. "Joint Custody Through Mediation Reviewed." *Conciliation Courts Review* 26: 53–58.

Buchanan, C., E. Maccoby, and S. Dornbusch. 1997. *Adolescents After Divorce*. Cambridge, MA: Harvard University Press.

CanWest News Service. 2003. "Janice Tibbetts, Justice Minister Rejects Idea of Joint Custody in Proposed Divorce Laws." March 28.

Capaldi, D., M. Forgatch, and L. Crosby. 1994. "Affective Expression in Family Problem Solving with Adolescent Boys." *Journal of Adolescent Research* 9: 28–49.

Cawson, P. 2002. Child Maltreatment in the Family. London: NSPCC.

Chase-Lansdale, P.L., A.J. Cherlin, and K. Kiernan. 1995. "The Long-Term Effects of Parental Divorce on the Mental Health of Young Adults: A Developmental Perspective." *Child Development* 66, 1614–34.

Corcoran, K., and J.C. Melamed. 1990. "From Coercion to Empowerment: Spousal Abuse and Mediation." *Mediation Quarterly* 7(4): 303–16.

Corneau, G. 1991. *Absent Fathers, Lost Sons*. Boston: Shambhala.

Crowder, K., and J. Teachman, 2004. "Do Residential Conditions Explain the Relationship Between Living Arrangements and Adolescent Behavior?" *Journal of Marriage and Family* 66: 721–38.

Daly, M., and M. Wilson. 1988. *Homicide*. New York: Aldine de Gruyter.

Dawson, D.A. 1991. "Family Structure and Children's Health and Well-Being." *Journal of Marriage and the Family* 53: 573–84.

Department of Justice Canada. 1990. *Evaluation of the Divorce Act, Phase II: Monitoring and Evaluation*, Ottawa: Minister of Justice.

Derevensky, J.L., and L. Deschamps. 1997. "Young Adults from Divorced and Intact Families: Perceptions About Preferred Custodial Arrangements." *Journal of Divorce and Remarriage* 27: 105–22.

Dienhart, A. 2002. "Make Room for Daddy." *Journal of Family Issues* 22: 973–99.

Dodds, C. 2005. "Life Goes On: A Model of Long-Term Family Intervention for High Conflict Post-Divorce Relationships." Unpublished MSW major essay, University of British Columbia, School of Social Work and Family Studies.

Doherty, W.K., E. Kouneski, and M. Erickson. 1998. "Responsible Fathering: An Overview and Conceptual Framework." *Journal of Marriage and the Family* 60: 277–92.

Drill, R.L. 1986. "Young Adult Children of Divorced Parents: Depression and the Perception of Loss." *Journal of Divorce* 10 (1/2).

Dudley, J. 1996. "Noncustodial Fathers Speak About Their Parental Role." *Family and Conciliation Courts Review* 34.

Eardley, T., and M. Griffiths. 2009. *Non-resident Parents and Service Use*. Sydney: Social Policy Research Centre, University of New South Wales.

Elliott, J., and M. Richards. 1985. "Parental Divorce and the Life Chances of Children." *Family Law* 19: 481–84.

Ellis, B.J., et al. 2003. "Does Father Absence Place Daughters at Special Risk for Early Sexual Activity and Teenage Pregnancy?" *Child Development* 74: 801–21.

Ellis, D., and L. Wight-Peasley. 1986. "Wife Abuse Among Separated Women." Paper presented at the meeting of the International Association for the Study of Aggression, Chicago.

Ellis, E.M. 2005. "Help of the Alienated Parent." *American Journal of Family Therapy* 33: 415–26.

Ely, M., P. West, H. Sweeting, and M. Richards. 2000. "Teenage Family Life, Life Chances, Lifestyles and Health: A Comparison of Two Contemporary Cohorts." *International Journal of Law, Policy and the Family* 14: 1–30.

Emery, R. 1994. *Children of Divorce*. New York: Guilford.

Fabricius, W. 2003. "Listening to Children of Divorce: New Findings that Diverge from Wallerstein, Lewis, and Blakeslee." *Family Relations* 52(4): 385–96.

Fabricius, W., and J.A. Hall. 2000. "Young Adults' Perspectives on Divorce: Living Arrangements." *Family Court Review* 38(4): 446–61.

Fabricius, W., and L. Luecken. 2007. "Postdivorce Living Arrangements, Parent Conflict, and Long-Term Physical Health Correlates for Children of Divorce." *Journal of Family Psychology* 21(2): 195–205.

Fabricius, W., et al. 2010. "Custody and Parenting Time: Links to Family Relationships and Well Being after Divorce." In M.E. Lamb (ed.), *The Role of the Father in Child Development*. Fifth edition. Cambridge: Wiley.

Family and Work Institute. 2007. *Family and Work Trends*. New York: Family and Work Institute.

Father Inclusive Practice Forum. 2005. *Principles of Father-inclusive Practice*. Newcastle: Father Inclusive Practice Forum.

Flood-Page, C., S. Campbell, V. Harrington, and J. Miller. 2000. *Youth Crime: Findings from the 1998/99 Youth Lifestyles Survey*. London: Home Office Research, Development and Statistics Directorate.

Fournier, F.. and A. Quéniart. 1995. «Paternités Brisées: Trajectoires de Pères en Rupture de Contact avec Leur Enfant.» In R.B. Dandurand et al., *Enfances: Perspectives Sociales et Pluriculturelles*, sous la direction de IQRC, Québec: 173–86.

Frost, A., and B. Pakiz. 1990. "The Effects of Marital Disruption on Adolescents: Time as a Dynamic." *American Journal of Orthopsychiatry* 60(4).

Furstenberg, F. Jr., C.W. Nord, J.L. Peterson, and N. Zill. 1983. "The Life Course of Children of Divorce: Marital Disruption and Parental Contact." *American Sociological Review* 48: 656–68.

Garber, B. 2004. "Directed Co-Parenting Intervention: Conducting Child-Centered Interventions in Parallel with Highly Conflicted Co-Parents." *Professional Psychology: Research and Practice* 35(1): 55–64.

Graham, J., and B. Bowling. 1995. *Young People and Crime*. London: Home Office.

Green, S. 2003. "Reaching Out to Fathers: An Examination of Staff Efforts that Lead to Greater Father Involvement in Early Childhood Programs." *Early Childhood Research and Practice* 5(2).

Gunnoe, M.L., and S.L. Braver. 2002a. *The Effects of Joint Legal Custody on Family Functioning*. Washington, DC: National Institute of Mental Health.

_____. 2002b. "The Effects of Joint Legal Custody on Mothers, Fathers, and Children Controlling for Factors that Predispose a Sole Maternal Versus Joint Legal Award." *Law and Human Behavior* 25(1).

Hawthorne, B., and C.J. Lennings. 2008. "The Marginalization of Nonresident Fathers: Their Postdivorce Roles." *Journal of Divorce and Remarriage* 49 (3/4): 191–209.

Hetherington, E.M. 2002. *For Better or Worse: Divorce Reconsidered.* New York: Norton.

Hetherington, E.M., M. Cox, and R. Cox, R. 1978. "The Aftermath of Divorce." In J.H. Stevens, Jr. and M. Mathews (eds.), *Mother-Child, Father-Child Relations.* Washington: National Association for the Education of Young Children.

Higgins, C., and L. Duxbury. 2002. *The 2001 National Work-life Conflict Study.* Ottawa: Health Canada.

Hope, S., C. Power, and B. Rodgers. 1998. "The Relationship Between Parental Separation in Childhood and Problem Drinking in Adulthood." *Addiction* 93(4): 505–14.

Hotton, T. 2003. "Childhood Aggression and Exposure to Violence in the Home." *Crime and Justice Research Paper Series.* Catalogue no. 85-561-MIE2003002. Ottawa: Statistics Canada, Canadian Centre for Justice Statistics.

Jaffe, P., C.V. Crooks, and N. Bala. 2005. *Making Appropriate Parenting Arrangements in Family Violence Cases: Applying the Literature to Identify Promising Practices.* Ottawa: Department of Justice Canada.

Jaffe, P., N. Lemon, and S.E. Poisson. 2003. *Child Custody and Domestic Violence: A Call for Safety and Accountability.* Thousand Oaks: Sage.

Jeynes, W.H. 2000. "A Longitudinal Analysis on the Effects of Remarriage Following Divorce on the Academic Achievement of Adolescents." *Journal of Divorce and Remarriage* 33: 131–48.

_____. 2001. "The Effects of Recent Parental Divorce on Their Children's Consumption of Marijuana and Cocaine." *Journal of Divorce and Remarriage* 35(3/4): 43–64.

Johnson, H., and T. Hotton. 2003. "Losing Control: Homicide Risk in Estranged and Intact Intimate Relationships." *Homicide Studies* 7(1): 58–84.

Kalter, N. 1987. "Long-Term Effects of Divorce on Children: A Developmental Vulnerability Model." *American Journal of Orthopsychiatry* 57(4).

Kelly, J.B. 1997. "The Best interest of the Child: A Concept in Search of Meaning." *Family and Conciliation Courts Review* 35(4): 377–87.

_____. 2000. "Children's Adjustment in Conflicted Marriage and Divorce: A Decade Review of Research." *Journal of the American Academy of Child and Adolescent Psychiatry* 39: 963–73.

_____. 2006. "Children's Living Arrangements Following Separation and Divorce: Insights from Empirical Research." *Family Process* 46(1): 35–52.

_____. 2007. "Children's Living Arrangements Following Separation and Divorce: Insights from Empirical and Clinical Research." *Family Process* 46(1): 35–52.

Kelly, J.B., and R.E. Emery. 2003. "Children's Adjustment Following Divorce: Risk and Resilience Perspectives." *Family Relations* 52: 352–62.

Kelly, J., and M. Lamb. 2000. "Using Child Development Research to Make Appropriate Custody and Access Decisions." *Family and Conciliation Courts Review* 38: 297–311.

Kelly, R.F., and S.L. Ward. 2002. "Allocating Custodial Responsibilities at

Divorce: Social Science Research and the American Law Institute's Approximation Rule." *Family Court Review* 40: 350–70.

Kiernan, K. 1997. *The Legacy of Parental Divorce: Social, Economic and Family Experiences in Adulthood*. London: Centre for Analysis of Social Exclusion, London School of Economics.

Kposowa, A. 2000. "Marital Status and Suicide in the National Longitudinal Mortality Study." *Journal of Epidemiology and Community Health* 54(4): 254–61.

_____. 2003. "Divorce and Suicide Risk." *Journal of Epidemiology and Community Health* 57: 993–95.

Kruk, E. 1989. "The Impact of Divorce on Non-Custodial Fathers: Psychological and Structural Factors Contributing to Disengagement." Unpublished Ph.D. thesis, University of Edinburgh.

_____. 1993. *Divorce and Disengagement*. Halifax: Fernwood.

_____. 2005. "Shared Parental Responsibility: A Harm Reduction-Based Approach to Divorce Law Reform." *Journal of Divorce and Remarriage* 43(3/4): 119–40.

_____. 2010a. "Parental and Social Institutional Responsibilities to Children's Needs in the Divorce Transition: Fathers' Perspectives." *Journal of Men's Studies* 18(2): 159–78.

_____. 2010b. "Collateral Damage: The Lived Experiences of Divorced Mothers Without Custody." *Journal of Divorce and Remarriage* 51(7/8).

Lamb, M.E. 1999. "Non-custodial Fathers and Their Impact on Children of Divorce." In Ross A. Thompson and Paul R. Amato (eds.), *The Post-Divorce Family: Research and Policy Issues*. Thousand Oaks, CA: Sage.

_____. (ed.). 2004. *The Role of the Father in Child Development*. Fourth edition. New York: Wiley.

Lamb, M.E., C. Hwang, and R. Ketterlinus. 1999. "Parent-Child Relationships." In M. Bornstein (ed.), *Developmental Psychology: An Advanced Textbook*. Fourth edition. Mahwah, NJ: Lawrence Erlbaum.

Lamb, M.E., and J. Pleck. 1985. "Paternal Behavior in Humans." *American Zoologist* 25: 883–94.

Lamb, M.E., K. Sternberg, and R.A. Thompson. 1997. "The Effects of Divorce and Custody Arrangements on Children's Behavior, Development, and Adjustment." *Family and Conciliation Courts.Review*, 35.

Lansdale, L., A. Cherlin, and K. Kiernan. 1995. "The Long Term Effects of Divorce on the Mental Health of Young Adults." *Child Development* 66: 1614–34.

Laumann-Billings, L., and R.E. Emery. 2000. "Distress Among Young Adults from Divorced Families." *Journal of Family Psychology* 14(4): 671–87.

Lebow, J. 2003. "Integrative Family Therapy for Disputes Involving Child Custody and Visitation." *Journal of Family Psychology* 17(2).

Lee, Jeff. 2000. "Family Blames Justice System for Pushing Man to Suicide." *Vancouver Sun*, March 23.

Levine, J.A., and E.W. Pitt. 1995. *New Expectations: Community Strategies for Responsible*

*Fatherhood.* New York: Families and Work Institute.

Liete, R.W., and P.C. McKenry. 2002. "Aspects of Father Status and Postdivorce Father Involvement with Children." *Journal of Family Issues* 23: 601–23.

Lohr, R., A. Mendell, and B. Riemer. 1989. "Clinical Observations on Interferences of Early Father Absence in the Achievement of Femininity." *Clinical Social Work Journal* 17(4).

Lund, M. 1987. "The Non-Custodial Father: Common Challenges in Parenting after Divorce." In C. Lewis and M. O' Brien (ed.), *Reassessing Fatherhood.* Newbury Park, CA: Sage.

Lundbert, O. 1993. "The Impact of Childhood Living Conditions on Illness and Mortality in Adulthood." *Social Science and Medicine* 36: 1047–52.

Marshall, K. 2006. "Converging Gender Roles." *Perspectives on Labour and Income* 7(7), 5–16.

Mason, M.A. 1994. *From Father's Property to Children's Rights.* New York: Columbia University Press.

McCue Horwitz, S., et al. 2003. "Language Delay in a Community Cohort of Young Children." *Journal of the American Academy of Child and Adolescent Psychiatry* 42: 932–40.

McMunn, A.M., et al. 2001. "Children's Emotional and Behavioural Well-Being and the Family Environment: Findings from the Health Survey for England." *Social Science and Medicine* 53: 423–40.

Meltzer, H., et al. 2000. *Mental Health of Children and Adolescents in Great Britain.* London: Stationery Office.

Milke, M. 2004. "The Time Squeeze." *Journal of Marriage and Family* 66: 739–61.

Nielsen, L. 1999. "Demeaning, Demoralizing, and Disenfranchising Divorced Dads: A Review of the Literature." *Journal of Divorce & Remarriage* 31(3/4): 139–77.

Nord, C.W., D. Brimhall, and J. West. 1997. *Fathers' Involvement in their Children's Schools.* Washington: U.S. Department of Education.

O'Neill, R. 2002. *Experiments in Living: The Fatherless Family.* London: civitas.

Office for National Statistics. 2001. *Mortality Statistics: General, Review of the Registrar General on Deaths in England and Wales, 1999.* Series DH1 32, Office for National Statistics.

Ontario Women's Network on Custody and Access. 2001. "Brief to the Federal, Provincial, Territorial Family Law Committee on Custody, Access and Child Support." Toronto: Ontario Women's Network on Custody and Access.

Parish, T.S. 1987. "Children's Self Concepts: Are They Affected by Parental Divorce and Remarriage?" *Journal of Social Behavior and Personality* 2(4): 559–62.

Parkinson, P., J. Cashmore, and J. Single. 2005. "Adolescents' Views on the Fairness of Parenting and Financial Arrangements After Separation." *Family Court Review* 43(3): 429–44.

Pleck, J.H. 1997. "Paternal Involvement: Levels, Sources, and Consequences." In M.E. Lamb (ed.), *The Role of the Father in Child Development.* Third edition.

Hoboken, NJ: Wiley.

Power, C., B. Rodgers, and S. Hope. 1999. "Heavy Alcohol Consumption and Marital Status: Disentangling the Relationship in a National Study of Young Adults." *Addiction* 94(10): 1477–87.

Rees, G., and C. Rutherford. 2001. *Home Run: Families and Young Runaways*. London: Children's Society.

Ringbäck Weitoft, G., et al. 2003 "Mortality, Severe Morbidity, and Injury in Children Living with Single Parents in Sweden: A Population-Based Study." *The Lancet* 361: 289–95.

Rosenberg, J., and W.B. Wilcox. 2006. *The Importance of Fathers in the Healthy Development of Children*. Washington: U.S. Department of Health and Human Services.

Special House of Commons-Senate Committee on Child Custody and Access. 1998. *For the Sake of the Children*. Ottawa: Government of Canada.

Statistics Canada. 2005. *Divorce in Canada: A Statistical Profile 2005*. Ottawa: Minister of Industry.

_____. 2011. *Family Violence in Canada: A Statistical Profile*. Ottawa: Minister of Industry.

Sweeting, H., P. West, and M. Richards. 1998. "Teenage Family Life, Lifestyles and Life Chances: Associations with Family Structure, Conflict with Parents and Joint Family Activity." *International Journal of Law, Policy and the Family* 12: 15–46.

Tucker, J.S., H.S., Friedman, J.E., Schwartz, and M.H. Criqui. 1997. "Parental Divorce: Effects on Individual Behavior and Longevity." *Journal of Personality and Social Psychology* 73: 381–91.

Wallerstein, J. S. and Kelly, J. 1980. *Surviving the Breakup: How Children and Parents Cope with Divorce*. New York: Basic Books.

Warshak, R.A. 1992. *The Custody Revolution*. New York: Simon and Schuster.

Wellings, K., J. Field, A.M. Johnson, and J. Wadsworth. 1994. *Sexual Behaviour in Britain*. London: Penguin.

Wellings, K., K. Nanchanahal, and W. MacDowall. 2001. "Sexual Behaviour in Britain: Early Heterosexual Experience." *The Lancet* 358: 1843–50.

Williams, J., and H. Boushey. 2010. *Three Faces of Work-family Conflict*. Washington, DC: Institute for American Progress.

Winslow, S. 2005. "Work Family Conflict and Gender: 1977–1997." *Journal of Family Issues* 26: 727–55.

# NEW in the Basic Series
# from Fernwood Publishing

## Sex and the Supreme Court
### Obscenity and Indecency Law in Canada

*Richard Jochelson & Kirsten Kramar*

9781552664155 $17.95 112pp Rights: World March 2011
Canadian laws pertaining to pornography and bawdy houses were first developed during the Victorian era, when "non-normative" sexualities were understood as a corruption of conservative morals and harmful to society as a whole. Tracing the socio-legal history of contemporary obscenity and indecency laws, Kramar and Jochelson contend that the law continues to function to protect society from harm. Today, rather than seeing harm to conservative values, the court sees harm to liberal political values. While reforms have been made, especially in light of feminist and queer challenges, Kramar and Jochelson use Foucault's governmentality framework to show that the liberal harm strategy for governing obscenity and indecency continues to disguise power.

RICHARD JOCHELSON is a professor of criminal justice at the University of Winnipeg. KIRSTEN KRAMAR is a professor of sociology at the University of Winnipeg.

## False Positive
### Private Profit in Canada's Medical Laboratories

*Ross Sutherland*

9781552664094 $17.95 128pp Rights: World March 2011
When your doctor takes a blood sample for analysis, where does it go? Does it find its way to your local, publicly owned hospital? Does it take a longer journey to a private, for-profit lab in the next city? Chances are, you've never given it a lot of thought. In this daring exposé of the laboratory system, Sutherland investigates its historical and contemporary development in Canada and argues that the landscape has been heavily influenced by the private, for-profit companies — to the detriment of the public health care system.

ROSS SUTHERLAND is a registered nurse and holds a master's degree in political economy from Carleton University.

visit www.fernwoodpublishing.ca for the complete list of the Basics Series

# ALSO NEW IN 2011

## Gendered Intersections
An Introduction to Women's and Gender Studies, 2nd Edition

*C. Lesley Biggs, Susan Gingell & Pamela Downe, eds.*

pb 9781552664131 $54.95 hb 9781552664292 $74.95 424pp Rights: World May, 2011 (short discount only)

Following the structure of the successful first edition of *Gendered Intersections*, this second edition examines the intersections across and between gender, race, culture, class, ability, sexuality, age and geographical location from the diverse perspectives of academics, artists and activists. Using a variety of mediums — academic research, poetry, statistics, visual essays, fiction, emails and music — this collection offers a unique exploration of gender through issues such as Aboriginal self-governance, poverty, work, spirituality, globalization and community activism. This new edition brings a greater focus on politics, and gender and the law. It also includes access to a Gendered Intersections website, which contains several performances by poets and a Gendered Intersections Quiz, which highlights the historical and contemporary contributions of women and non-hegemonic men on Canadian Society.

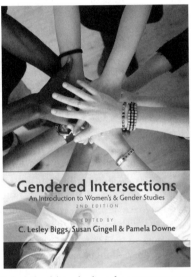

Praise for the first edition

"*Gendered Intersections*' diverse selections provide an excellent and encompassing overview in the field of Women's and Gender Studies in Canada today. The thought-provoking readings encourage students to use a gendered perspective to engage in a critical analysis of current issues and topics. I find this an excellent text to get students thinking about the gendered world in which live."
— *Wendee Kubik, Women's Studies, University of Regina*

C. LESLEY BIGGS is an associate professor in the history department at the University of Saskatchewan. SUSAN GINGELL is a professor in the Department of English at the University of Saskatchewan. PAMELA DOWNE is an associate professor and head of the Department of Archeology and Anthropology at the University of Saskatchewan.

visit www.fernwoodpublishing.ca for the complete list of new titles

# ABOUT CANADA SERIES

About Canada explores key issues for Canadians. Accessibly written, affordable and in a distinctive format, these books provide basic — but critical and passionate — coverage of central aspects of our society.

## About Canada: Immigration

*Nupur Gogia & Bonnie Slade*
pb 9781552664070 $17.95
hb 9781552664315 $34.95
144pp Rights: World March, 2011

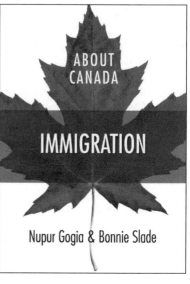

Many Canadians believe that immigrants steal jobs away from qualified Canadians, abuse the healthcare system and refuse to participate in Canadian culture. In *About Canada: Immigration*, Gogia and Slade challenge these myths with a thorough investigation of the realities of immigrating to Canada. Examining historical immigration policies, the authors note that these policies were always fundamentally racist, favouring whites, unless hard labourers were needed. Although current policies are no longer explicitly racist, they do continue to favour certain kinds of applicants. Many recent immigrants to Canada are highly trained and educated professionals, and yet few of them, contrary to the myth, find work in their area of expertise. Despite the fact that these experts could contribute significantly to Canadian society, deeply ingrained racism, suspicion and fear keep immigrants out of these jobs. On the other hand, Canada also requires construction workers, nannies and agricultural workers — but few immigrants who do this work qualify for citizenship. *About Canada: Immigration* argues that we need to move beyond the myths and build an immigration policy that meets the needs of Canadian society.

NUPUR GOGIA received her PhD in sociology and equity studies in education at OISE, University of Toronto. BONNIE SLADE is a research fellow with the Institute of Education at the University of Stirling in Scotland.

visit www.fernwoodpublishing.ca for the complete list of About Canada titles

## About Canada:
## Youth and Children

*Bernard Schissel*
pb 9781552664124 $17.95
hb 9781552664346 $34.95
144pp Rights: World May, 2011

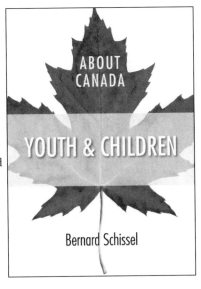

Canada is a signatory on the United
Nations Declaration of the Rights of the
Child, which guarantees the protection and
care of children and youth. *About Canada:
Children and Youth* examines each of the
rights within the Canadian context — and
finds Canada wanting. Schissel argues that
although our expressed desire is to protect
and care for our children, the reality is
that young people, in Canada and around
the world, often lack basic human rights.
The lives of young people are steeped in abuse from the education and justice
systems, exploitation by corporations, ill health and poverty. And while the hearts
of Canadians go out to youth in distant countries suffering under oppressive
circumstances, those same hearts often have little sympathy for the suffering of
youth, particularly disadvantaged youth, within Canada. This book explores our
contradictory views and argues that we must do more to ensure that the rights of
the child are upheld.

BERNARD SCHISSEL is a professor in and head of the Doctor of Social
Sciences Program, Faculty of Social and Applied Sciences, Royal Roads
University.

visit www.fernwoodpublishing.ca for the complete list of About Canada titles